MW01104419

THE
7|8|9
MARRIAGE

7 Rules, 3 Tools. Simplified Communication
Secrets Healthy, Happy Couples Use to
Stay Consistently Close

GLADE DANIELS-BROWN
WITH ROMAN DANIELS-BROWN

7|8|9

This publication is designed to provide accurate and author-itative information in regard to the subject matter covered. It is sold with the understanding that the publisher is not engaged in rendering legal, mental health, or other professional service. If legal advice or other expert assistance is required, the services of a competent professional should be sought.

The techniques described in this book are not a substitute for medical or psychiatric treatment. If you are dealing with in-dividuals who are mentally ill or may be a danger to you or to themselves, seek professional support immediately.

Names of clients, patients, organizations, and other identify-ing details have been altered to protect their privacy.

Acknowledgements

To our wives, Evelyn and Jessica, whose support and love never falter.

To Kim Greenburg, whose editing and encouraging friendship pushed this work to completion.

To Janae Hone and Shalene Lybbert, whose excellent work, friendship, and support make my work enjoyable.

To the designers at 99 designs for their exceptional work and creativity.

Dedication

I dedicate this book to my mother, whose belief in me made me believe in myself.

Contents

Foreword

My dad started writing this book because he felt a growing sense of obligation to get this vital information out. It quickly became a monkey on his back, the same way LeBron James had to win a championship in Cleveland before he felt indisputably proven. My dad just had to write this book.

Not only did he think that the tools and principles presented here could help couples, but he also got tired of hearing the bull that is out there. Seriously, there is so much misinformation regarding how to deal with common marital communication problems that it's bizarre. Dad would incessantly rant at and argue with the T.V. whenever a "marriage expert" uttered things such as "Swinging can be the answer to problems in bed," or "You need to learn to fight fair," or, his personal favorite, "To deal with your marital issues, you need to sit down together and express your deepest feelings." Through decades of working with couples, he learned that most of them were not that interested in "exchanging deep feelings" all the time. In fact, most of his marital clients come to him because they are frustrated and tired of other therapists always asking them "How does that make you feel?" It makes them nuts. It makes him nuts.

Dad knows that many couples do enjoy sitting and sharing feelings to their hearts' content while camping in the woods, but most of them probably don't need therapy to teach them how to communicate. He's in the other camp of communicators: those who want to efficiently communicate and then get on with their lives, while still feeling close to their spouse.

Dad frequently reports that he works with amazing couples who have taught him much about marriage. More than half of what you will find in this book has been taught to him by couples he's interacted or counseled with. He often shares things like, "This really great couple taught me _____". I'm going to use this idea with all my couples." Dad consistently finds his job interesting and inspiring; he has truly found his niche.

This book contains the 20% of lean content that will lead to 80% of daily marital success. Together we have vetted this book to cut through the moderately useful stuff and provide you with the top things couples need to learn for quick, and mostly painless, results. It's been a great joy writing and laughing together as we compiled *The 7-8-9 Marriage*. Every son should have such a chance with his dad.

– Roman Daniels-Brown

Introduction

"To love rightly is to love what is orderly and beautiful in an educated and disciplined way."
– Plato

A great marriage that lasts is at the top of the list for most men and women. Unfortunately, most people never achieve this type of marriage. It's not because they lose interest in having a great marriage; rather, it's because they don't fully know *how* to have one.

A great marriage is a 7-8-9 marriage. What does this mean? On a scale of 0 to 10, when it comes to feeling close to your spouse, what's your number? Your spouse's number may be different from yours. Not to worry. An honest number is all you need to consider right now. A "10" represents feeling extremely close and connected, and a "0" represents feeling completely distant from your spouse. If you are a typical couple, it's likely you have felt many of the in-between numbers.

This book will teach you how to have a consistent 7-8-9 marriage by using and following specific rules and tools as you communicate. No more sudden drops from a 7 to a 2. No more trips and dinners spent in conflict or silence. No more doubt and despair as you ask yourself, "Did I make a mistake when I married this person?" These negative experiences and feelings will significantly decrease or end. A strong, connected relationship with your spouse will become reality. Both of you will make it happen.

Most people believe love is the key to having a great relationship. This is false. I often hear one spouse ask another, "Why do you keep acting this way or behaving like that toward me if you love me?" Love *is* required as a foundation of marriage. However, skills are necessary to build a solid structure on that foundation. That structure you will build is closeness.

This book will give you the tools and principles you need to have a consistently excellent marriage through better communication. Many people say to me, "I wish I would have known about this before I even started dating." Yeah, me too, but it will get better from here! Choosing the right person to marry definitely helps your cause.

To have an excellent marriage, you must follow certain rules and acquire some tools. Without these rules and tools, you will likely end up with a poor, 0-1-2-3 marriage or an average, 4-5-6 marriage, like the majority of the population. You don't want to settle for those numbers when a 7-8-9 marriage is what you really want and need!

When I was a young boy, my grandma told me, "Glade, marriage is daily work." (She and Grandpa must have been fighting that day.) She was correct in her counsel. What she didn't clarify was that marriage can be daily *hard* work or daily *easy* work. A great marriage that lasts is daily easy work. Unhappy marriages expend time and energy on daily hard work.

Have you ever heard someone say, referring to their spouse, "I love him, but I'm not *in* love with him"? I've never liked that phrase, but frankly, what this person is really saying is, "I love him, but I don't feel close to him."

This book explains how to have closeness-focused communication. By communicating in this way, you will build on your foundation of love and have a close and connected marriage. You will have a relationship that other couples will look at and say, "I want what they have!" Any other kind of marriage is just plain hard work!

When you follow the rules and use the tools outlined in this book, I promise you will experience rapid improvements in your marriage. These improvements will be lasting, you will know how to handle problems as they come, and you will no longer feel lost and confused. I have witnessed it thousands of times. A 7-8-9 marriage is wonderful, and it is achievable.

To get the most out of this book, it is imperative that you read and understand the chapters that precede the rules and tools chapters. These chapters will help you understand the need to follow the rules and use the tools while talking to your spouse. The equation I will help you to understand, when followed with exactness, will not disappoint. When followed consistently, I've never seen it fail.

The world often sends the message that marriage sucks, but I affirm that marriage can be awesome for everyone who wants a great one. You are to be commended for your effort to have a better relationship with your spouse. You are great just for that effort alone.

Chapter 1

The 0 to 10 Scale of Closeness

*"Whatever you think about persistently
tends to happen to you eventually."*
— Anonymous

How do you begin this whole process? First, both you and your spouse should rate yourself on a scale of 0 to 10 of how close you feel to each other. Healthy couples regularly scale their feelings of closeness verbally with each other. Unhealthy couples have no idea what their spouse's number is. They haven't even considered it, or they guess. They may not talk about their numbers because they want to avoid contention. They may also be afraid of the answer. This scale is a quick measurement of how close you feel to your spouse, not how much you love him or her, although love is a component of that closeness. A scale simplifies a potentially lengthy discussion of your overall closeness. This quick assessment acts as an alert to inform each other of your current status.

SCALE OF CLOSENESS

0,1,2,3,4,5,6,7,8,9,10

So, on a scale of 0 to 10, if you were to rate your overall closeness with your spouse, what would your number be? "0, I'm completely distant", or, "10, I'm extremely close." Be honest with your spouse and yourself. Be objective. There's no need to debate the number. It is just an honest assessment, at this time, of how you are feeling. There should be no pretending, exaggerating, or dramatizing your actual closeness. These numbers will be your starting point. By the way, there is no -1 or exaggerated 11. Changing numbers over time is not a sign of failure. Changing numbers simply means your closeness with each other fluctuates over time. 7-8-9 couples learn to discipline, restrict, and limit these movements.

Don't be afraid of your number or your spouse's number. You may be a bit nervous to hear their number, but in a healthy marriage, partners honestly assess where they are. When you hear your spouse's number, do not be defensive. Just let it be for the moment. Unhealthy couples ignore or deny where they are on the scale and often fudge their numbers to play games or to leverage their spouse to change. Healthy couples don't play games. They feel safe telling each other their honest number and know they won't be chastised, harassed, or ridiculed for that number. You will both eventually be a 7-8-9 together, so start with respectful, honest scaling.

⚬

Scaling Ethics

#1. Don't play games during the scale number selection.

Choosing a number in order to gain an upper hand against your partner will degrade the assessment. Example: *"I'm a 4 and you're an 8? Looks like you owe me!"* No game playing. Don't do it.

#2. Don't react negatively, at least outwardly. Relax. This is not an emergency.

While hearing numbers from your spouse may invoke instinctual hurt, fear, or anger, take care not to react in a way that will hurt your spouse. Healthy couples are completely respectful of their spouse's honest scaling. A respectful response would be, "Thank you for telling me. Let me think about that for a bit to see what I need to improve on, and we can talk later about our numbers."

#3. Don't be evasive; be honest.

Don't say, "I haven't really thought about it," or "I'm a 7" just to avoid your spouse's disappointment or to avoid contention. Honesty is attractive to 7-8-9 couples.

#4. Remember, your numbers will change.

It may be discouraging to face the reality of saying "2" to your spouse, or hearing a "1" or "0" from your spouse. But have faith and do not fear. The numbers will move upward if you choose to follow the rules and tools in this book.

Building closeness from a foundation of love requires a quick and simple measuring tool. If the measurement is not quick and simple, couples will make it complex, confusing, and messy as they use lengthy descriptions of how they feel. These lengthy descriptions begin to cause serious communication problems. You don't need algebra to count pocket change. The 0 to 10 scale is an effective measuring tool you can use regularly throughout your marriage. Most people love the simplicity of this technique. Remember, this is just an assessment; it isn't the time to pull out the pick and shovel and go to work. This is simply to help you become more aware of your relationship status at this moment. It's natural to become inquisitive at this point, but please resist the urge to fix the number. Just relax and breathe. You'll become an expert on your spouse soon enough.

Throughout this book, I will refer to couples as *"healthy"* or *"unhealthy."* Unhealthy is a 0-5 level, and healthy is a 6-10 level. You have probably felt that your marriage has been both healthy and unhealthy at times. A smart marriage requires regular self-assessment. The healthiest marriages maintain a 7-8-9 rating. They drop only to a 6 level, and they have moments of a 10. Fluctuations are to be expected, and within that range, fluctuations can be managed. A 6 and a 10 are most likely short-lived. This is typical of healthy, happy couples. 7-8-9 is the sought-after and desired range in which to stay.

This scale of closeness can effectively be used for the duration of your marriage. It is essential that you regularly measure where you are and check in with your spouse to see where they are in terms of closeness with you. "What's your number today?" is a simple way to ask. I have been asked many times what "regular" means. It depends, but for the average couple in the beginning of their change process, I would suggest two to three times per week. As your marriage becomes more solid, I would suggest a weekly check-in. Do it more often if it's helpful, less if it's annoying.

Checking in with each other is similar to parents checking on their young child in a swimming pool. Healthy couples have high awareness and show loving concern. They are interested in the well-being of their loved one and show this with vigilance, but they are never controlling.

Unhealthy couples are apathetic, neglectful, and self-interested. They have low awareness of their spouse's experience in the relationship. When the children are in the pool, they are taking a nap.

When you know your number and your spouse's number, you can focus on moving toward a consistent 7-8-9 relationship. Regular, daily awareness is extremely important to 7-8-9s. Wouldn't you feel good knowing your spouse has high awareness of your numbers? Assessing your own and your spouse's numbers will help you become experts on each other. 7-8-9 couples seek this consistent expertise. When you feel mired in details or confused by the latest and greatest contradictory advice, return to this short chapter. All you need to remember is to follow the scaling ethics.

⋗ ONE MORE THOUGHT

After hearing your spouse's number – a 5, for example – simply ask them, *"What can I do to help you move to a 6 or 7?"* Most responses require only a simple, inexpensive fix. I frequently hear, "Just hold my hand more often," or "Kiss me like you used to." One wife said with a smile, "Please shave and shower before we go out."

You know what moves your numbers up. Teach your spouse with exactness what that is. Guessing is for middle school crushes. There's nothing much cooler than your spouse asking you how they can make you and your marriage feel better. How's that for a thought? Despite what you might think, your spouse actually wants you to be happier!

Chapter 2

0-3, 4-6, 7-9 Marriage Traits

"A good system shortens the road to the goal."
– Orison Swett Marden

arriages fall into three different ranges on the 0-10 scale. I have observed that about 30-40% of couples fall within the 0-3 range of closeness. These miserable couples are barely surviving. They feel there is little hope for change. Discouraged and tired, they are often looking for a way out. They will say, *"I can't keep doing this anymore."* The embers of love and connection have all but gone out for them. This is often where affairs occur. The problems feel severe.

. Communication explosions occur. Each partner tries to solve problems on their own, without their spouse. Both are living parallel lives of loneliness. This is when couples enter marital therapy to give it one last try. They are in deep trouble and need immediate help.

Traits of a 0-3 Miserable Relationship

1. Barely surviving
2. Looking for a way out of the marriage
3. Attempting to solve problems alone
4. Overall sense of misery and resentment toward each other

Another 40-50% of couples fall into the 4-6 range. These couples have what I call a "roommate" relationship. They are apathetic and have decided that trying to work on specific, important marital issues is too troublesome. They feel even worse after trying to talk about important issues in their relationship. They do what they can to avoid those conflicts. They are not miserable, but they are not fulfilled in their relationship, and they long for more connection. They like the relationship overall but want improvements.

When conflicts occur, they are afraid of creating more distance, so they keep quiet or get upset internally. When they can't tolerate their internal upset feelings any longer, they become aggressive and agitated when speaking. They are scared to move down the closeness scale, so they remain complacent. They have lost hope of becoming closer. They are in a state of mediocrity. This marital state is often what they observed in their parents' relationships. In counseling these couples, I often hear, "I guess this is as good as it gets" or "Living with my spouse is like living with a sibling." These statements are often followed by "I guess this is marriage," or "It just doesn't feel right." They are correct. It isn't right.

Traits of a 4-6 Roommate Relationship

1. Apathetic and no longer hopeful the relationship will improve
2. Talking about problems makes them worse or doesn't change anything
3. State of mediocrity
4. Spouses *"tolerate"* each other

The last range is a 7-9 marriage. About 10-20% of couples fall in this range. These couples are close and connected. They are happy and feel fulfilled with their spouse. They have a good balance between independence and a quality connection.

They support and respect each other. They don't engage in drama, compete with each other, or play games. They have high integrity. They are individually refined. They assume the best about each other. They laugh. They cry safely.

7-8-9s are predominately happy and content in their marriage. They are not perfect and they make errors, but they are not punished by their spouse for these errors. They are close and they love each other at the same time. They want to be together and grow old together.

Traits of a 7-9 Healthy, Happy Relationship

1. Close and connected
2. High respect for each other
3. No drama
4. Positive assumptions about each other
5. Want to be together and grow old together

3 RANGES OF CLOSENESS

(0,1,2,3)	(4,5,6)	(7,8,9)	(10)
MISERABLE RELATIONSHIP	ROOMMATE RELATIONSHIP	HEALTHY HAPPY RELATIONSHIP	BLISSFUL MOMENTS

Don't get discouraged with where you are on the scale. As you learn and apply the rules and tools outlined in this book, you will see progress and have renewed optimism for your relationship. Having a 7-8-9 relationship is a process. When you follow the process, progress will come. Progress will bring arousal for you and your spouse. I have never seen a couple be disappointed with a progressing spouse or relationship. Together you will build wonderful closeness.

A great marriage is obtainable; however, it requires learning new tools and following set rules. It requires work, but this work is exciting. Working to be close is always the objective. As you find your desire and commit yourself to permanent change, your relationship will flourish. As you maintain high awareness of your numbers, you will navigate your relationship to a consistent 7-8-9 level.

What are the typical barriers to achieving a 7-8-9 marriage?

1. Pride
2. Resistance
3. Stubbornness
4. Fault finding

If you have any of these problems, it is crucial that you become humble enough to change. To be humble means you become meek and submissive, even teachable. Your spouse will find these traits in you attractive, not weak. You want your spouse to find you attractive, right? Then find your humility.

⮂ ONE MORE THOUGHT

Use your spiritual belief or core belief system to find your humility. It will be pretty tough to have a consistent 7-8-9 marriage without that internal compass.

Do not listen to people who tell you that having a sustained 7-8-9 relationship isn't possible or is just too hard. Those individuals lack what it takes or have never read this book and consistently applied its system. Join your lives with other couples who are trying to have a great life. It's okay to let go of couples who pull you down like a crab in a bucket.

When you are able to achieve a 7-8-9 marriage, share your success and the information you have learned with everyone! Teaching the skills will help them become more deeply ingrained in your own relationship. What a great feeling it will be when you help your good friends achieve their 7-8-9.

Chapter 3

Commit Yourself

*"An ounce of performance
is worth pounds of promises."*
– Mae West

When a couple comes in to therapy, they are nearly always fatigued. They have tried everything in their arsenal of skills, and they have lost hope that their relationship can get better. They have tried to copy what other couples do. They have read articles and books. They have complained to coworkers or friends. These efforts have failed or were inadequate. They are so miserable and defeated in their marriage that even going to therapy sounds less horrible than what they've been doing.

Other couples come in because they have sensed a decline in their relationship and are trying to do "damage control" before it becomes too messy. Good for them. It's always better to catch the problem before it worsens. Preventive work is better than major reconstruction later.

Sometimes both parties are willing to participate in therapy but are equally confused about what to do about their problems. They are looking for guidance. Often, one person comes in, dragging the reluctant spouse. Sometimes they come in to a session with one of them hoping the therapist will advise them to end the marriage or tell their spouse to shape up. Regardless of the reasons, they are close to losing their commitment to continue trying, or their marriage is hanging by a thread.

With the exception of situations that involve abuse, domestic violence, or severe addiction, the vast majority of marriages can be revived and strengthened to a 7-8-9 level. Even marriages that struggle with the devastation of an affair, leaving them at a 0-1 level, can have a 7-8-9 marriage.

One client wrote about a tragic experience in which her husband had an affair. The couple came in to therapy at a 1-2 level. They used the skills and moved their way up the scale over a number of months. With her permission, I share her note:

> "I had been seeing Glade Daniels-Brown for a couple of months when I had my "10" moment. I had found out that my husband of 29 years had had an affair fifteen years earlier. I was having a hard time with it because I never thought it would happen to me. We had been working really hard on our numbers using the techniques. We became a 7-8 most of the time. One night we were intimate. I was so relaxed and I just felt one with my husband. I was so close to him, not just sexually or physically, but emotionally and spiritually. It was amazing! I can't remember when I had felt like that before. I know it won't be like that every time, but I'm so looking forward to the next 10."

Now, I can teach you the rules and tools of a 7-8-9 marriage, but there is one thing I cannot give you. That is the *desire* to change and to achieve a 7-8-9 marriage. If there is no desire, there will be no commitment. Potential 7-8-9 couples who have a desire will see their commitment increase and their motivation build as they follow the rules and apply the tools explained in this book. Desire for change is like the engine of a train, and the commitment is the caboose. If you lead with the desire, commitment will naturally follow. Even if you only have a desire to have a desire, you are in a good starting place. If you have any desire to have a 7-8-9 marriage, you are off to a great start! You can increase desire by disciplining your negative thoughts and thinking good things about your spouse. There are good things, you know. Nurturing your desire will sprout hope in both of you. Your spouse will feel it from you.

You may find yourself working on this endeavor alone. Your spouse may not want to read or invest the time to explore new "techniques." You can find comfort in the fact that even if you are the only one using the rules and tools outlined here, remarkable changes will come. I have found that in a marriage, even if just one person is dedicated to change, the other party will warm up and join the effort. As a therapist, I am often providing marriage counseling with only one client in the room. The other person just couldn't or wouldn't start the process. Great things happen when a new direction begins with either one or two people.

One of the remarkable changes that I see happen in therapy is when a wife or husband turns to the other and says, "I really want to try to have a great marriage with you. Do you want that with me?" When they both agree, it's a wonderful surge to their action steps. Without commitment, there's very little movement up the closeness scale.

To help you commit yourself to a better relationship, there are a few facts I will share with you about your spouse.

1. They have a deep desire to be wanted, as do you.
2. They have a strong desire for you to be interested in them.
3. They want you to think of them.

So, in a nutshell, your spouse wants to be desired and pursued. In later chapters, I will give you the tools to fulfill these wants of your spouse with exactness. Pay attention and follow the script. Find your desire to change and to become closer to your spouse, and be firm in that commitment. Your relationship is too important to take casually.

⤳ ONE MORE THOUGHT

When you work on your marriage, be confident in the direction you are headed as you work toward your 7-8-9 marriage. I've watched too many couples who are indecisive, uncommitted, or only semi-committed. Some do the least they can and put forth limited effort to change. They want to see what happens; they want to test whether their spouse will reciprocate. 7-8-9 couples are fully committed.

A proactive and enthusiastic couple will progress much faster than a passive or uninterested couple. If you have decided to get in, then get in. Don't mess around. Be a little more like Tigger and a little less like Eeyore as you reconcile your relationship. You know what I mean.

Chapter 4

The #1 Marital Problem

*"Being alone is scary, but not as scary
as feeling alone in a relationship."*
— Amelia Earhart

I consider it a privilege to have worked with and assisted thousands of couples in marital therapy. I am often asked, "What is the main reason couples come in to therapy?" The answer is quite simple. No, it's not money or sex or problems with in-laws. It's not pets, building a house together, or too much football watching. These are the identified problems, but they are not the actual problem.

The number one reason couples come in to therapy is that they are not feeling close to each other anymore. They once had love and closeness, and they miss the way they felt then. They don't understand why the closeness is missing or how to get it back. They feel separate and detached. They are working hard to find that elusive closeness, but it's not working. They used to share their thoughts, feelings, and emotions with each other. Now they keep these things to themselves. Instead of growing closer, they are moving away from each other. They feel allergic to each other.

When one couple came in to our first session, the wife explained, "When we were first married, we had a little apartment. We loved the coziness of our small place. Now, 15 years later, we have a 5,000-square-foot home, and that doesn't even seem to be enough space away from each other." I laughed, but it obviously wasn't funny. How sad to think about what this couple once had and how, to them, it had mysteriously evaporated. They were a perfect example of a couple who loved each other but who no longer felt close to each other.

Have you felt this way? Has some of your closeness evaporated over time? This can change. There are significant differences between 0-5 couples and 6-10 couples. Awareness and technique will bring desired change. They will bring closeness once again, consistent closeness, maybe to a level you've never experienced before.

A marriage without closeness is lonely and miserable. Couples in this kind of marriage are always seeking for connection but repeatedly being disappointed. You are done with this. You have felt the feelings of disconnect, rejection, fear, and hurt thousands of times. You want these bad feelings to end, but you don't want to end the marriage. As you use the rules and tools we will discuss, you and your spouse will find the stable closeness you have been seeking.

Now, you may be thinking to yourself, "No, it's not a matter of closeness; it is these issues that are the problem, and if we can just get those resolved, then we will be close again." Maybe so, but why aren't you getting those issues resolved? You also may be thinking to yourself, "I have an unmotivated spouse, and I've tried everything to get him/her to change, so of course we're not close." Yes, that's a pain, but everyone has a need, and you may not have tapped in to that need yet.

Various other reasons may cause you to resist moving forward. It makes sense that you may be fatigued or just tired of trying. Start new and let's get your marriage going in the right direction. You've done hard things and made it through. You have a reserve tank, and I want you to flip on the switch. I'm going to show you the easier way.

Start today with the puppy tip below. It's one of the first assignments I give couples before we even begin to work on communication.

When your spouse comes home, act like a puppy that runs and greets its owner. Go toward your spouse, wag your tail, and connect. Look at them, smile at them (yes, I believe puppies smile), and touch them. It's infectious. I'm telling you right now. If you have stopped doing this—going toward your spouse— then you are bringing on much of your own pain and misery. I'm simply encouraging you to do what you used to do. True?

Don't let your resistance, stubbornness, or resentment dominate your actions. The simple gesture of sincerely connecting with your spouse will be instantly delicious to your relationship. So if you are throwing a tantrum and trying to punish your spouse by not connecting with them, stop it. Relinquish your pride and start healing yourself and your marriage. You'll both feel better with just a few minutes of effort.

If you are a cat lover, greet your spouse by lying on your back and twisting side to side until they pet you. I've never tried it, but it just might work!

Chapter 5

The Principle of Deterioration

"To cease to admire is proof of deterioration."
– Charles Horton Cooley

hy does marriage seem so hard? Well, the simple answer is the most accurate. Most things deteriorate. A house, a car, a tin can, and our bodies all deteriorate over time. Marriage is no different. Unless you and your spouse are actively working on your relationship closeness, you will deteriorate as a couple. The main reason marriages crumble is because couples fatigue as they experience life stresses such as work, children, finances, in-laws, and other obligations. They get sick, hungry, angry, and lonely. Just by themselves, the negative aspects of individual personalities mixed together can cause plenty of deterioration. When problems come, couples attempt to communicate about the problems and all the other challenges of living. Often their communication fails, and deterioration increases. When deterioration increases, closeness decreases. Love may stay completely intact, but without closeness, love loses its potency.

I sort of enjoy telling engaged couples about the principle of deterioration. They just stare at me as if I know nothing about the power of their new love. I know they are thinking, "Yeah, but we're different." What a shock it is to them when they find out they really aren't any different from the rest of us. When they realize they need to be actively engaged in their marriage and not just engaged to be married, they learn that deterioration is manageable.

It's healthy to tell a young couple about the principle of deterioration before they marry. It keeps them from feeling there is something wrong with them when distance occurs. It's important for all couples to understand deterioration so they can stop blaming their spouse and work together to combat deterioration.

I once told a very young couple about the principle of deterioration during a pre-marital counseling session. The young woman looked at me, almost frightened, and asked, "You mean we're probably going to end up divorced!?"

"No, of course not," I replied, "Deterioration happens to all couples." Healthy couples manage deterioration. Unhealthy couples do not. Knowing how to manage deterioration is a powerful skill that 7-8-9 couples are aware of and respect. Most people struggle with the hidden problem of deterioration for one reason. Nobody taught them about any of this. Let's talk a little more about how deterioration begins.

During courtship, an underlying problem develops. Since the man's and the woman's lives have not been completely joined together at this point, they tend to ignore or set aside their issues to enjoy the bliss of new love and attraction. They enjoy the 7-8-9-10 feelings of closeness and don't want them to end. Who wants to derail that experience when it feels so wonderful? These wonderful feelings, arousal, and closeness could be described as a 7-8-9 relationship. It's often short-lived, however, due to the necessity of dealing with the troubles of life. These troubles come upon a couple quickly as they get closer to joining their lives together. The joining of two lives is a miracle in action. The foundation of love is an essential fuel to make it through this transition. All too often, when deterioration begins to creep in, people will say, "Well, the honeymoon is over."

Poor communication habits are at the core of deterioration. Over time, what happens to a couple's communication? The couple begins to focus on resolving issues rather than focusing on closeness. This births a negative change — sometimes permanent — in their communication culture. It causes a couple to fight or not talk about things that are important to them. This is huge! This shift away from a focus on closeness to a resolution focus is what causes many couples to eventually separate or divorce. This is often the chief complaint of the couples I work with. If a couple doesn't learn to reverse this negative pattern, they will settle for a less-than-fulfilling relationship or completely end the relationship. Too often I see people who love each other end their marriage simply because they do not know how to change this pattern. A necessary reversal of this communication pattern will be discussed in chapter 8, The War/Quit Cycle. It's critical to study this chapter and implement the change.

The principle of deterioration in marriage can be compared to a river that never stops flowing. A couple dealing with deterioration can be represented by two salmon swimming upstream against the river's current. They must continue swimming because the troubles and issues never stop coming. They must swim side by side, together. They must have high awareness of and actively support each other. They must find each other daily, or they will naturally drift apart. They must do these things, for the life of the 7-8-9 marriage depends on it.

THE PRINCIPLE OF DETERIORATION

$$(0,1,2,3) \quad (4,5,6) \quad (7,8,9) \quad (10)$$

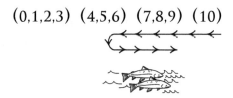

Although side-by-side swimming is ideal, sometimes one person expends additional energy and moves just ahead of the other to break current if the other is feeling weak. Often the husband and wife change positions and provide relief for the other. On occasion, one works at 90% efficiency and the other at 10% because of illness or hardship. At another time, one person may be giving 60% and the other 40%.

But shouldn't both people be putting in 100% all the time? In Utopia, they should and would. But in the real world of healthy, happy 7-8-9 couples, *"fair"* means the constant change and fluctuation of individual time and energy in the relationship, with both putting forth their best effort. 7-8-9 couples switch off willingly for the benefit of the whole. They're not keeping track of everything they do. This is known as being a help-meet for each other. They help meet the troubles the marriage and family face. If they quit swimming or putting forth effort, then the current of problems will wash one or both of them away, and they will lose closeness and connection with each other. Unfortunately, this happens often for many couples. But it doesn't need to.

Deterioration in marriage is sort of like deterioration in the cars we drive. Do you like driving a car that is dirty inside and out? I don't. It affects my mood in a negative way. A car's cleanliness deteriorates naturally. My neglect and messiness probably contribute the most. Driving a car that has deteriorated doesn't make me feel my best. I don't think my passengers enjoy it much either. However, when I wash and vacuum my car, clean the windows, and freshen it up, I feel much better. It's better to clean my car regularly than to have to pay once a year to have it completely detailed. Keeping the car clean takes just a little time and targeted work, and my whole attitude about it improves. Marriage is just like this. When it has deteriorated a bit, it doesn't take too much to make it feel better. Hey, even my passengers would agree with this analogy.

Simple Definition: Deterioration means that if something is left alone or neglected, it will erode and decay. Marriage is no different.

Healthy couples recognize that deterioration is a given in the relationship and not a dysfunction. They understand that deterioration can't be controlled, but it can be managed. They learn to manage communication deterioration in a functional way using the rules and tools of a 7-8-9 marriage.

Healthy couples allow deterioration to drop their level of closeness only to a 6 before reversing the downward trend. This is critical. They quickly swim upward together when they notice this drop. 7-8-9 couples never allow deterioration to bring them to a 0-5 level. A 0-5 ceases to be an option for 7-8-9 couples. They know they need to manage deterioration rather than letting deterioration manage their marriage. 7-8-9s use high awareness and the 0-10 scale of closeness to assess deterioration before it becomes unmanageable. They go toward each other with support when they see it happening.

Unhealthy couples lack the rules and tools to manage deterioration. Often, they contribute to deterioration by acting out at each other. One person may turn tail and swim downstream because he or she lacks the discipline or just doesn't have the skills to deal with difficulties at the time. This person assumes that doing it alone will work better. But in most cases, the hardships increase when people go solo.

Deterioration that is out of control or not managed in a marriage is sad to watch. Remember, deterioration is always happening, so you must always be swimming together. Swimming together means staying focused on closeness more than on the deteriorating problems. A couple who is close is strong. That couple will withstand the toughest currents of deterioration that come their way. Yes, deterioration is a problem for couples, but it can definitely be managed.

Strategies to Manage Deterioration

1. Focus on being close, and regularly use the 7-8-9 scale to see what your spouse's number is.

2. When you know your spouse's number, ask what you can do to make it move up a number or two. Actively work on these things right away.

3. Focus on not doing things that agitate or frustrate your spouse. You know what these things are because your spouse has probably told you a few times.

4. Make these changes part of your new permanent self. Change the culture of your relationship by being solid in your personal change. This change should include going toward your spouse in support, rather than away from them in frustration.

⮩ ONE MORE THOUGHT

Marriage is the greatest institution for joy and happiness in the world. Why would you allow it to deteriorate if it truly is that valuable? Aside from your core belief system or spiritual beliefs, nothing affects your life more than the state of your marriage. Nothing.

Deterioration, not your spouse, is the enemy. Now that you recognize or re-recognize deterioration as a potential negative power in your marriage, work to protect it, as 7-8-9 couples do. You are The Terminator reprogrammed, deterioration is the Cyborg, and your marriage is Sara Connor. Here's your mission. It's urgent. Check in with your spouse a couple more times a day than you normally do. Make your husband or wife feel wanted by you. Protect your spouse and be willing to do whatever it takes so both of you can be close. Your marriage is counting on you. You are strong!

Chapter 6

The Head, Heart, and Stomach Gauge

"Listen to your intuition.
It will tell you everything you need to know."
– Anthony J. D'Angelo

What is the best gauge for recognizing when your marriage is deteriorating? Your Head, Heart, and Stomach. These physical and emotional triggers help you know where you stand with regards to closeness with your spouse. The Head, Heart, and Stomach gauge tells unhealthy couples they are not doing well and tells healthy couples they are doing well. Yes, it's your marital intuition gauge to help you scale your closeness. When an individual is feeling unhealthy with their spouse, their head is full of negative thoughts about them. Their heart feels distant and it hurts, and their stomach feels uneasy when they think of their spouse. When an individual is feeling healthy with their spouse, their head is at rest, and they have good thoughts about their spouse. Their heart feels warm and close, and their stomach is calm and at ease.

The Head, Heart, and Stomach gauge is accurate. It's yours. You will need to learn to trust it to identify your closeness numbers. Most couples have felt the feelings on both sides of the scale at some point in their marriage. This is why I tell couples that having a 0-5 relationship is hard work in your head, heart, and stomach. Having a 6-10 relationship is easy work in your head, heart, and stomach. Trust the internal gauge. It will save your marriage from unnecessary pain and suffering.

In addition to the Head, Heart, and Stomach gauge, other feelings and behaviors are indications of an unhealthy or healthy marriage. Unhealthy couples have dominant warning traits of their 0-5 relationship. Healthy couples have dominant confirming traits of their 6-10 relationship.

There are three main traits on each side of the 0-10 scale that identify the health of a marriage. Of course, there are more traits, but it is unnecessary to dissect every trait to recognize your current number on the 0-10 scale of closeness. A quick and simple assessment will tell you a lot. Here are the traits of unhealthy couples.

1. They are scared of each other.

They experience a great deal of fear. They say things like the following:

"I'm afraid that if I talk about this issue, she will get mad."
"I'm afraid things will get worse than they already are."
"I'm afraid he doesn't love me."
"I'm afraid she will leave me."
In the worst-case scenario, a spouse may say, "I'm afraid he will hit me or cheat on me."

They think negatively about their spouse and assume that their spouse is doing less than they can, or that they want to make their life uncomfortable. They predict negative reactions from their spouse. They prepare themselves for these reactions by being defensive and, at times, aggressive.

2. They intentionally hurt each other.

"He's not being nice, so I'm not going to be nice."
"She doesn't say she's sorry. I'm not saying I'm sorry."

They name call or use the silent treatment. They emotionally wound and are critical of each other. They completely ignore each other or they act or talk in a condescending way. They show contempt or sarcasm when they communicate.

They use toxic speech: "I'm so tired of listening to your stupid comments!"

They use exaggerated phrases: "You never do anything I ask or listen to anything I say!"

They throw out immature, trendy, and dramatic words: "Whatever," "Really?" "Seriously!?"

In a nutshell, they tantrum when they speak to each other. When they are fighting, they act just like middle school students!

3. They are just surviving.

When a husband and wife are at a 0-5 level of closeness, they don't eat as well, sleep as well, work as well, vacation as well, or celebrate the holidays as well. They feel sick. Their head is constantly thinking about the negative aspects of their relationship. Their heart hurts and feels broken. Their stomach is in knots and feels uneasy. It's not a feeling they want. As the saying goes, "Hurt people hurt people."

They are losing or have lost one another and are not swimming together in closeness anymore. They feel miserable. To avoid feeling victimized in their relationship, they begin to handle problems on their own. They subconsciously, and sometimes consciously, fantasize about getting out of the marriage. They are in trouble.

Healthy couples experience the opposite in their marriage. As a 6-10 couple, they enjoy their marriage. Here are the traits of healthy couples.

1. Healthy couples have faith in each other.

They feel good about their spouse and assume the best of them. They give each other the benefit of the doubt. They have confidence in their spouse's ability to improve. In talking about her husband, one wife explained, "I never worry about what my husband does when I'm not with him because he has integrity." She assumes the positive of her husband because he has earned her trust.

Healthy couples trust that their spouse holds the same or similar goals for their future. Each spouse really likes the other. They smile when they see each other. This inner faith in each other propels them toward each other. They are consistent in using the tools and following the rules in this book. They know they must.

2. They may hurt each other, but that hurt is unintentional.

When there is a misunderstanding, healthy couples often say, "Oops, I'm sorry I hurt you, but that was not my intent."

6-10 couples work toward healing the marriage; it is never their intent to hurt each other. They are not interested in punishing or retaliating against their spouse. They don't harbor resentment.

3. Their heads, hearts, and stomachs are at rest.

Their heads are filled with good thoughts. Their hearts feel warm and are yearning to show love. Their stomachs are relaxed. They consistently feel close to their spouse. They eat well, sleep well, work well, vacation well, and celebrate the holidays well. They are swimming together. They don't want these feelings to end, so they continually assess where they are and focus their energy on maintaining this closeness. These are the rewards of working together.

Summing it up, it is quite obvious how both sides operate. Of course, there are other traits we could discuss, but these are enough to "self-diagnose" to see if you are on the right track.

Unhealthy couples	Healthy couples
0-5 traits	6-10 traits
Fear	Faith
Intent	Error
Surviving	Thriving
Hard work	Easy work

If you are on the lower end of the scale of closeness, how can you make the transition to a higher number? What should you work on to make a 7-8-9 happen?

Start by taking a courageous risk. Deny your negative assumption and replace it with a positive assumption. For example, instead of thinking, "My wife will probably reject my sexual advances this weekend," I can take a courageous risk and change my thinking and behaviors. I can choose instead to be positive by showing affection, and maybe this weekend will be pleasurable for both of us. Write your own script and fill it. If it doesn't work this time, continue to take positive risks. 7-8-9s continually take courageous, positive risks.

Remember to give your spouse the benefit of the doubt. You didn't choose a loser. You chose a person you wanted to thrive with. They wanted to thrive with you. That person is still in there. Yes, they may have become a little distracted with life or have some annoying habits, but they are changeable. They need some nudging and encouragement to be their best self. They want to be their best self for you. Invest your time and energy into helping them aspire higher. Don't hurt them with your tantrums and reactive behavior. Ease their head, heart, and stomach, and they will want to reciprocate.

I love this quote by Marvin J. Ashton:

> "If we could look into each other's hearts and understand the unique challenges each of us face, I think we would treat each other much more gently, with more love, patience, tolerance and care. Be one who nurtures and who builds. Be one who has an understanding and a forgiving heart, who looks for the best in people."

Isn't this true? Don't you wish your spouse would carry this kind of awareness toward you? Even if they don't, you can with them.

Another great quote explains this idea in a much shorter version: "A little consideration. A little thought for others makes all the difference." (Eeyore, *Winnie the Pooh*)

⇗ ONE MORE THOUGHT

Hey, listen up! When you were dating, you used to pay attention to almost everything your girlfriend or boyfriend was doing. You had high-resolution glasses on to watch them. You thought about them much of your day. You had fantasies about them. They occupied a lot of your mental time and energy, and you loved it. No, you weren't a stalker. You were a pursuer.

You used to want to have the best relationship there was. (I think you still do.) You loved the thought of having that kind of relationship with them. Your head, heart, and stomach were completely invested! You may have forgotten this. Now it's time to remember and resurrect this attitude.

I promise you that it's not as complicated as you may have made it. It's not as complicated as other couples tell you it is. Ask yourself, "Are my head, heart, and stomach in the right place to secure a 7-8-9 relationship again, or to achieve that kind of relationship for the first time?"

If not, change your mindset and figure it out! The rules and tools outlined in this book will take you there. Remember, desire and humility are essential. Consistent use of the rules and tools will be the key to your success. This is not a short-term task. It is a long-term pleasure. I know you are looking for this kind of happiness.

Chapter 7

The Failed Communication Goal of Unhealthy Marriages

*"The framing of a problem is often
far more essential than its solution."*
– Albert Einstein

W hen two people meet and begin to date, they are on their best behavior. They work to present their optimal selves. They show their least flawed side and do what it takes to secure their connection with each other. However, they can sustain this presentation only for a brief time. (Sticking one's chest out and sucking in one's gut has time limitations.) They are trying to assess their love and compatibility. Yes, they are completely checking each other out. If they choose to pursue each other, they have decided it is worth committing more time and energy. Nice work.

However, the longer the couple dates, the more their negative differences naturally appear. These differences become harder and harder to ignore, threatening their current infatuation and budding love.

As they continue their courtship, problems arise more often. These include family conflicts, sexual incompatibility, spirituality differences, past unresolved problems, and phone or device usage. The shift from mostly pleasure to occasional pain begins to surface. Deterioration has already begun. The couple is now in a difficult spot. They have problems that need to be addressed. They believe the problems need to be resolved so they can feel better, but attempting to resolve the problems results in contention. Contention can threaten how they currently feel. The feeling that is in jeopardy is their 7-8-9 experience. They have even felt some 10 moments. They really like those! So when conflict arises, they must ask themselves, "Is it worth the risk of contention to address the underlying problem?"

Maybe this couple has tried and succeeded in working through some of their problems. Other problems, maybe not. They try to "shelve" these other issues so as to not threaten their 7-8-9 relationship. "We'll deal with those later," might be their plan. Even better, they hope, "Maybe these issues will resolve themselves."

As time goes on, more frustrations surface because the couple's best behavior evaporates. Some unlikable behaviors become more obvious. Repetition of these relationship frustrations leads to agitation. Deterioration of the relationship closeness accelerates. Some of these agitations have become explosions or are nearing explosions. Multiple failed attempts to hint frustrations away have increased each person's frustrations and agitations. As a result, the couple's closeness often deteriorates to a 0-5 range. And here we go. The Head, Heart, and Stomach gauge is triggered.

One great couple I worked with (and I only work with great couples) likened these drops of closeness to an aggressive teeter-totter experience. The wife said, "We start off working together on the task, but then all of a sudden we start fighting, and someone jumps off the teeter-totter, and the other one slams hard to the ground. That's what it feels like every time!"

So what's a couple to do with these frustrations, agitations, and explosions? Most couples think the simple solution is to fix the problems that have caused distance. They erroneously believe that if they can resolve all their problems, they will feel close and connected. They believe that resolution of issues will re-establish peace and happy feelings in their relationship. I wish that were true. I've tried it myself.

UNHAPPY COUPLES' COMMUNICATION PATTERN

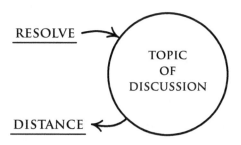

But this is where the main dysfunctional pattern begins. Don't get me wrong; I believe resolving some issues in marriage is essential. However, the vast majority of issues in a marriage *do not need to be resolved.* You're going to like that part. Remember, some things are intolerable and absolutely require change—for example, addictions, affairs, domestic violence, or other serious, harmful behaviors.

This erroneous expectation—that if couples can resolve their problems, they will feel close—is a common one. For example, a sharp mother of three came in to a session and told me, "I'm working full-time and attending school full-time, and I recently remarried. My husband has three kids of his own. The reason I'm here is to ask a question: What can I do to make all our children get along? They don't like each other at all." Then she said, "If we could just resolve this problem, our whole lives would be much better. We might even have a baby together. Hopefully, this would make me and my husband feel fully connected." This woman's focus on resolution was hopeful and idealistic, but it was nonetheless in error. Resolving current problems by adding more "connecting" problems does not result in closeness.

A focus on resolution sets the stage for a conflict scenario that can last for decades. I'll detail this War/Quit cycle clearly in the next chapter.

I have worked with thousands of couples who, through no fault of their own, have fallen into this error of resolution focus. They didn't want to be stuck in this cycle; it just kind of happened while they were trying to solve their problems. It's sad to watch. On the other hand, it's wonderful to watch them change right in front of me when they learn and begin to use simple skills. It *is* possible to change, and the change is sustainable.

Couples ask me all the time, "Why didn't anyone explain this to me before I got married, or even when I was dating!?"

My answer? No one explains this because everyone is trying to figure it out themselves — everyone except the long-time happily married couples, that is. What happens when you ask these older couples, "Grandma and Grandpa, what's the secret to a long-lasting marriage?" Everyone quietly waits for the answer.

The old unhappy couples sometimes say, "I worked outside and she worked inside. That kept us from fighting," or, "I learned to just put up with a lot of things to make it work."

One unhappy couple told me, "We never divorced because we never decided to divorce at the same time." Now there's a great phrase to put on a 50th anniversary cake!

When happy couples are asked this question, they say things like this:

"We just tried to be good friends."
"We say we're sorry before we go to sleep."
"We think of our spouse more than ourselves."
"We say 'I love you' every day."

Everyone sighs and says, "Oh, that's so sweet."

Then they look at each other and ask their spouse, "Why don't you do that with me?" Real complicated, huh?

When unhealthy couples hear the answers of healthy, happy couples, they just end up feeling bad. They more than likely settled for a 0-3 miserable marriage, or a 4-5-6 roommate marriage. Poor folks. I really feel for them. That's hard work in their heads, hearts, and stomachs.

Older healthy couples focused on closeness and enjoyed their 7-8-9 marriage. Their heads, hearts, and stomachs felt at peace. Near the end of the book, we'll discuss veteran couples, and I'll identify their secrets, which will confirm everything you will read in this book.

By the way, I'll bet you have never heard one of these older 7-8-9 couples say, "You have to resolve all your problems to have a happy marriage."

But hey, don't just take it from me. Go ask some of these older couples yourself. I'll even give you the question to ask. "Mr. and Mrs. Clever, are all your issues resolved in your marriage?" I'd love to hear the answers you get. My experience has been that most happily married couples' issues are in the process of being dissolved or have evaporated over time. I've been fortunate to have gathered this wisdom from these veteran couples.

This marital manual supplies the skills, rules, and tools of a 7-8-9 relationship. You can use it as a constant resource when you've lost your way. These skills will always direct you upward with your spouse. Talk about these skills. Share them with your friends and family members. The more you do, the more they will become a permanent part of your new marital culture.

Without rules and tools to guide them, a couple may deteriorate to the point of divorce. They may abandon the relationship or live in a state of resentment and apathy. This does not need to happen, and the reality is that both of you want better.

Here's an interesting thing I have observed in therapy. At one point, most couples knew and used these skills. They used to follow the correct script at the beginning of their courtship, but when frustrations arose, they abandoned their natural, successful system. They abandoned their closeness focus and became resolution focused. Hello, deterioration.

Summed up, when a couple focuses on resolving problems as they discuss their issues, they are much more likely to deteriorate throughout their discussion. The heavy expectation to re-solve their concerns is overwhelming and exhausting for at least one person in the relationship. They act out, react, fatigue, and begin to tantrum when a resolution is not reached. Helplessness and hopelessness set in when they are unsuccessful.

What should a couple be focusing on then? Closeness. I tell couples all the time, "The front-end goal of every conversation with your spouse is to be close. The tail-end goal of every con-versation should always be to be closer than when you start-ed the conversation. The goal is never resolution." When a couple begins to change and to once again focus on closeness rather than on resolving problems, they change their whole communication pattern to one that 7-8-9 couples follow. This is a pattern of friendly communication.

Don't buy into the counsel that you need to "Fight fair." Don't be fooled into thinking you need to go through lengthy programs and seminars to "heal your marriage." You don't need 20 evaluation forms, questionnaires, and a week of sem-inars to figure out every aspect of your partner and how to work with all those differences. You know you and your spouse won't follow through or remember everything anyway. And don't believe that you need to sit in a therapist's office and cry as you express all your "I feel" statements until you become completely devoid of self-respect. Nope, Nope, Nope.

After working with and watching thousands of couples over the years use the 7-8-9 system, I am convinced that every couple has the capacity to work through any problem without professional intervention.

I often tell couples that most of what I am going to teach them will confirm what they think they know, but don't know for sure.

Yes, I provide new information and some rules and tools, but the couple's own rich marital experiences, both bad and good, have made them the best expert on their relationship.

I believe strongly in all couples' innate abilities, strengths, life experiences, and wisdom to navigate their unique relationship to success by using just a few rules and tools. The only time this system fails, as mentioned before, is when humility and desire are lacking, or when there is a significant mental health problem, addiction, or abuse. Some of these issues require a divorce or professional help for safety reasons, and sometimes for greater life satisfaction. But this is the exception, not the rule.

⌁ ONE MORE THOUGHT

If you are the resolver in the relationship, I'm putting you in charge of changing your marital communication pattern to one that is closeness focused rather than resolution focused. When I say in charge, I mean to lead.

Why should you be the one to lead in this change? It's because you love outcome. You want results. You are a doer. You also want an excellent relationship. You want it to run efficiently and smoothly, and frankly, you want it now. These tools will help you have the things I just mentioned. They won't guide you to resolutions. They will guide you to something much better. They will guide you to consistent closeness.

Couples who feel consistently close and connected will have serious power to successfully manage all their life challenges. Their issues will dissolve. If you knew that changing your focus to one of closeness, not resolution, would bring about these awesome results, would you be motivated to learn a better way?

58

From this point forward, I want you to act "as if" you were a 7-8-9. Act *as if* you want to be close to your spouse. Act *as if* you want to be closer at the end of every conversation than when you started the conversation. Act *as if* you want your spouse to be a 7-8-9 with you. Acting "as if" will then become reality. That new reality will become your new 7-8-9 marital culture.

What do you need to do to obtain this closeness with your spouse? If you think for a minute, a couple of ideas will come to mind. Write those ideas down. Act on those positive thoughts. It's not about resolving your issues; it's about working toward closeness with your spouse. Get going. You and your spouse deserve it.

Chapter 8

The War / Quit Cycle

"There was never a good war,
or a bad peace."
 – Benjamin Franklin

When a couple resorts to a resolution focus to deal with their problems, they rewrite their communication script, and it becomes dysfunctional. Typically, there is one individual in the relationship who is more likely to push this resolution pattern. It isn't gender-specific. It is led by the person who has the stronger philosophy that the solution to marital distance is to resolve problems. This approach might work if both people are on board and never act out, and if neither person displays emotion or personality. Yeah, we're talking about zombies or cyborgs. Aside from those zombie/cyborg couples, most couples will fall into a pattern I call the "War/Quit" cycle.

THE WAR / QUIT CYCLE

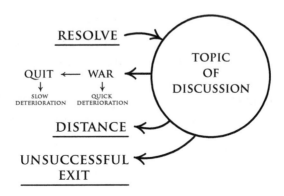

When a couple has a resolution focus, they feel pressure throughout their conversation: "We need to resolve this issue or we won't be close."

As they talk about the frustrating topic at hand, they become defensive. For example, they may differ on how to parent, how to manage finances, or whose mother they should live closest to. They feel they need to self-protect or defend their position. They argue with each other about what the solution should be.

This debate or argument is a kind of war. This war causes acute, or quick, deterioration. Each partner misbehaves or acts out during the discussion, and by the end, the couple has deteriorated on the scale of closeness. Now they feel lousy.

To avoid having another war, and in an attempt to preserve some closeness, they avoid or quit talking about the problem. They remember how bad they felt the last time they talked about this issue. They don't want to deteriorate further. However, this safeguard causes a new problem. Not talking about the issue causes chronic, or slow, deterioration.

The couple shelves the issue for another time, hoping the problem will go away. It doesn't. When the problem resurfaces, they remember that war isn't pleasant, but they are tired of not talking about it. They hope war won't happen this time. Great optimism! They attempt, again, to resolve the problem, only to find that a war breaks out, so once again, they quit talking about it. This dance continues dozens of times until they surrender to no or little change on that issue. I have listened to hundreds of stories from couples who, to avoid conflict, quit talking about an issue decades earlier.

I have observed that most couples have at least one or two "big" issues that fall into the war/quit cycle. Some of the main big issues that present in therapy are the need for sex and affection, anger, blended family issues, household responsibilities, addictions, and money.

Couples in the war/quit cycle are in a marital communication traffic jam. Paralyzed in their movement, they just honk their horn in frustration. They feel stuck. They struggle to find a way to get unstuck. When those attempts fail, they feel the marriage is failing. The result of falling into this war/quit cycle is not resolution of their issues, but deterioration of their closeness. They are now having thoughts such as, "I guess this is just the way it's going to be," or, "I can't talk to you about anything," or, "I can't live like this anymore."

These couples lose hope and faith in their ability to improve as a couple. They get discouraged about their future and are upset with themselves and each other. They begin to tantrum and misbehave in other aspects of their relationship. They aren't proud of these behaviors, but they just don't know what else to do. They have deteriorated to a 4-5-6 roommate status, or have dropped even lower to a 0-1-2-3 miserable status. They sure don't want to post this type of status on social media for the world to see. "Hey everyone, click 'like' if you are enjoying my miserable marriage!"

A couple I once worked with explained how they deteriorated. A quick and easy explanation, it summed up 90 percent of the couples I have seen. The wife said, "We used to get along. Now we don't. I don't know what happened." When couples process how their functional communication pattern became dysfunctional, from closeness focused to resolution focused, a light clicks on. They start to get excited when they learn that they can reverse this pattern. It's neat to see them get excited together. Joint excitement brings rapid changes.

The war/quit cycle must be recognized and confronted in order to change it. A new pattern using rules and tools must be implemented. This joint awareness gives the couple a common enemy that they can work to expel from their marriage. The old pattern must be destroyed.

The transition from a focus on closeness to a focus on resolution is a virus. The war/quit cycle is the outcome of the virus that too often infects a marriage. The solution is to clean out that virus and install the closeness-focused communication pattern. Once that virus is completely expelled, the marital relationship will run much more smoothly.

Hey, I know this can seem a little tricky. It might even seem illogical or strange. It does to me sometimes as I use the skills. Putting all that aside, I want you to hold on to my shirttail. Borrow some of my confidence and follow me on this one. This system, followed with exactness, works. Thousands of other couples have proven that it does. I tell couples in my office that they can achieve a consistent 7-8-9, and when they do, they can fire me. When they reach their 7-8-9 and I know they can sustain it, they do fire me. I've been fired hundreds of times by couples. I love being fired! A 7-8-9 relationship is SWEET!

⊰ ONE MORE THOUGHT

If you seek marital therapy, it should be brief. You need to be in therapy only between eight and fifteen sessions. On occasion, it may take a little longer. Continued "accountability" and "maintenance" visits are optional. If therapy is taking much longer than that, there's something wrong. If you're not progressing, it's because either you or your spouse aren't working. The therapist works for you. You should be directing therapy, not the therapist directing you.

I'm always amazed when a couple comes in for therapy and has no goals. Frequently they just want someone else to fix their marriage. It doesn't work that way. *You* fix you. *You* fix your marriage with your spouse's help. This book is your therapist. It won't fix your relationship—you will, through daily work.

7-8-9 couples work this system daily without coasting. They know deterioration will get the better of them if they become casual in their efforts. There's nothing of value in your life that didn't require serious sacrifice on someone's part. Your sacrifice of time and energy will be rewarded.

Sustaining a 7-8-9 relationship is easy work in your head, heart, and stomach. Having a 0-5 relationship is hard work in your head, heart, and stomach. Remember that? You will make mistakes. Big deal. It happens to all of us. I'll show you how to thoroughly clean up your mistakes in the tool section. No more pouting when it doesn't go your way. Take charge and make your marriage better with persistent effort.

Chapter 9

The Successful Communication Pattern of Healthy Marriages

"When I am with you, the only place
I want to be is closer."

– Unknown

You now know the solution to marital communication "traffic jams" known as the war/quit cycle. Yes, the solution begins with changing the front-end goal of every conversation. The tail-end goal is to be closer at the end of the conversation than when you started. Unhealthy couples focus on resolution. Happy, healthy couples focus on being close.

HEALTHY, HAPPY COUPLES'
COMMUNICATION PATTERN

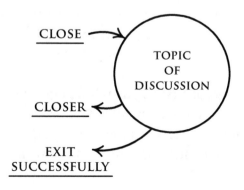

CLOSE

TOPIC OF DISCUSSION

CLOSER

EXIT SUCCESSFULLY

The shift may seem naïve, as if we are neglecting or are not concerned with the need for change. Not true. I love change. But I don't love going through a bunch of conflict or drama to get that change!

Conflict and drama are the primary causes of marital communication traffic jams, and the result is closeness deterioration. If you like conflict and drama when talking to your spouse, then do the opposite of everything I am suggesting. (Then again, if you like conflict and drama, I would suggest never marrying anyone, ever.) However, my guess is you really don't like conflict and drama. You just don't know how to work on things differently with that frustrating spouse of yours. More than likely, if you lead with correct technique, your spouse will follow your positive example.

I have observed this "leading" principle frequently when a client is willing to apply the techniques on their spouse. I mean "on," because using these techniques is like applying ointment on a wound. It begins the healing process. My counsel to you is to change yourself by applying the closeness technique throughout your conversations. Your spouse will follow your lead. It's not just communication patterns that need to be led; it's nearly anything you want to change in your marriage.

For example, one woman confided that her husband never showed any interest in her. She was quite attractive. I thought, "What's wrong with this guy that he could have such discipline as to deny his urges and not pursue his wife?"

After listening for just a little while, I learned that she was heavily involved in social media. She literally was looking at her phone for four to six hours a day. When her husband would come home from work, she would just sit there and sort of grunt when he came in. He'd make himself dinner – a bowl of cereal – and watch T.V.

I simply suggested that she apply a simple technique that would bring about a great change in him. She said, "Yeah, I know what you are going to say—sex, right?"

I said, "That may do it, but first use this simple primer technique."

Then I told her that the quickest way to elicit change in her husband was to greet him when she saw him. This may sound like a fluff technique. It's not. It is extremely powerful. I told her, "You will see reciprocation in just a few attempts as long as you use the proper 7-8-9 greeting. You must look at him (as if you like him), smile at him (as if you like him), and touch him (as if you like him) each time you greet him. It's that simple."

Unless a couple is completely emotionally dead with each other, greetings work 100% of the time. What does "work" mean? It means that genuine greetings will ignite a desire to move closer to each other. It means, "I like you. You like me. We can be a happy family." Everyone wants to be wanted and liked. Even more importantly, everyone needs to be wanted and liked.

So what's the rest of the story? The wife tried the technique. It worked. I later met with the husband. He was amazed at her therapeutic changes. When I asked him what he liked the most, he said, "For the longest time I felt like I was just living with her, kind of like a roommate. Now it seems like she is interested in me. It makes me want to be interested in her." Someone needs to lead the marriage to a 7-8-9. Why not you?

Back to the successful communication pattern of happy marriages. When I assert that closeness should be the goal of every conversation, it may feel too simplistic. That goal may feel hard to achieve with your spouse because of past communication failures. The techniques are simple. Controlling yourself and disciplining your reactions will be the challenge. As you follow the rules and tools, your self-discipline will increase. As your self-discipline improves, so will your closeness. The results you enjoy will be worth the energy expenditure.

It is possible for couples to change their resolution-focused dysfunctional pattern. It is possible for you, too! You just need a corrective nudge to remember something. Here's your nudge again. When you felt happy and connected, a focus on closeness was the basis of your communication. Most often this was at the beginning of your relationship, during your courtship. When problems began to surface, if you're like most couples, you slowly abandoned your closeness focus and became resolution focused in your communication.

I have worked with many couples who never had closeness-focused communication in their marriage or were never taught how to work through problems. They just followed what they observed from their parents' relationship(s), other people's relationships, or relationships they observed on T.V. Heaven help those couples. Most couples, however, have just forgotten how to communicate successfully. I'm attempting to remind you that you did correct things during your courtship. You just need a little encouragement to remember the good things you used to do. You have forgotten how to swim together against the river of deterioration.

When healthy, happy 7-8-9 couples start their conversation with a joint goal to be close while they talk, they relieve the front-end pressure to resolve their differences. When they do this, they relax. They change their experience before they begin to talk. They decide beforehand to behave and have a good, friendly experience. They follow a set of rules and use their tools. These rules and tools keep them safe. They have faith in their spouse and do not intend to hurt them. They want to thrive with and be closer to their spouse. They remember that having a 7-8-9 is why they are married.

When couples develop the habit of making every conversation closeness focused, a miracle begins to happen. What is this miracle? Their issues begin to dissolve. Keeping an eye on being closer at the end of the conversation than when they started the conversation keeps couples away from resolution thinking. Resolution focus is bad. Dissolving an issue is good. However, dissolving an issue is never the primary goal. It is always secondary to achieving closeness.

When couples keep these primary and secondary goals in their proper order, they do not fail. When they reverse the goals, and make resolving issues their primary goal, they often enter the war/quit cycle.

So what does it mean to *dissolve* an issue? Here are some definitions of dissolve:

> to melt
> to cause to disappear or vanish
> to break into component parts
> to disintegrate
> to lose intensity

Do not confuse *dissolving* an issue with *resolving* an issue. Couples who seek to *dissolve* issues work toward betterment and progress. For example, a couple who is struggling with intimacy may decide to start sitting next to each other in the evenings, instead of in separate chairs or in different rooms. On the other hand, if this same husband and wife are trying to *resolve* this issue, they might approach it like this: "I need you to be more affectionate so our sexual issues can get fixed once and for all."

Remember, maintaining closeness, rather than trying to resolve issues, is of critical importance. When 0-5 couples are resolution focused, it doesn't end well.

The following are some definitions of *resolve*:

to decide or determine firmly
to make up the mind of
to find the answer or solution
to bring to an end; conclude; to deal with conclusively

For healthy couples to remain in the 7-8-9 range, they need to be making progress. They need to see improvements. They need to have joint direction. They need changes so they won't be agitated or explode in order to get those changes. Greater growth, change, and progress happens for couples who keep closeness as their primary goal than it does for a couple whose primary goal is resolution.

Why is this? Because 7-8-9 couples end the war/quit cycle and the resulting acute and chronic deterioration that accompanies their conversations. When they keep their closeness focus, they gently dissolve their issues over time.

Their communication experiences become positive. This positive pattern of friendly experiences, with a focus on closeness, feels delicious. Couples seek to have more of that feeling, that 7-10 experience. They feel wonderfully close and are hopeful they can feel this way again. Even better, their sustained 7-8-9 level of closeness actually increases their desire to progress and grow. They want to talk about the issue another time because it was pleasant the time before. They remember why they liked each other in the first place.

If you are like the rest of us, you're more apt to perform better for someone who respects, likes, and is friendly with you versus someone who doesn't respect or like you. This may seem like common sense, but I witness this kind of bad behavior every day in my practice. Some couples literally have to be reminded to be respectful of each other and treat each other well. Watching two wounded people in the same room fighting to be liked, wanted, and respected is something everyone should experience. They both want the same thing—to be liked—but they end up hurting each other to achieve it. "Interesting," as Spock would say. Watching those same couples put into practice some simple techniques and become friendly in their communication is amazing.

When a couple maintains their relationship at a 7-8-9 level, their issues naturally melt, pass, disappear, vanish, disintegrate, and lose their intensity. When the issues are broken down into workable, manageable components following the rules and using the tools, those issues dissolve. The discussions become pleasant. Another way of saying this is the following:

Closeness is the recipe, the rules and tools are the ingredients, and the outcome is a delicious 7-8-9 (and sometimes a 10) experience with your spouse.

I tell couples they need to work on dissolving their issues, not their marriage. The rules and tools, followed with discipline, will keep you focused on this task.

To sum up this chapter:

- The front-end goal of every conversation is to be close.
- The tail-end goal of every conversation is to be closer than when you started the conversation.
- Do not be resolution focused.
- Dissolve marital issues over time by following the rules and using the tools.

⮞ ONE MORE THOUGHT

The more you move toward an excellent marriage, the more it will demand from you. A 7-8-9 is not a marriage of ease. It takes dedicated focus, drive, exactness, and daily grit. However, it's easy work—easy on your head, heart, and stomach.

7-8-9s exercise faith in their spouse and give them the benefit of the doubt. They tell their spouse daily that they notice the good things they are doing, and they resist the urge to nitpick and criticize. They play with each other and are happy to be together. They have high awareness of and want to make life easier for each other. Aside from their core or spiritual belief system, their spouse is their highest priority.

If you want a 0-5 marriage, simply relax. Your minimal efforts will get you there. Natural deterioration will assist you. Here's your recipe. Be critical; don't have fun. Assume the worst. Take your spouse for granted. Ignore their wants and needs and focus on yourself. There's more, but you get the point. Being in the 0-5 range is hard work; it's mentally taxing.

All marriages have various issues that will be dissolved to some extent over various time frames. Just remember that dissolving issues should not be your daily, primary focus;

closeness is. Dissolving means that the issue is not bothering you to the point of causing closeness deterioration.

Here's the hardcore reality. Brace yourself. Some issues take days, some weeks, months, years, decades, and yes, some take the rest of your life to dissolve. I know this after three decades of marriage; we still have issues that are in the dissolving process. But the key to a 7-8-9 marriage is feeling consistent love and consistent closeness, regardless of how long the issues take. Dissolving an issue is a process, not an end game.

As one couple told me, "We used to constantly look at all our problems and get completely overwhelmed and want to quit. Now we hold each other's hand, take a deep breath and say, 'Let's work it out together. It's so much easier when we're a team until we die.'"

One couple said, "Life is hard enough already without having to fight each other while going through it." I agree. On to the rules.

Chapter 10

Rule #1
Use Gentle Beginnings

"The expert at anything was once a beginner."
                                – Helen Keller

You need to be an expert 7-8-9 communication companion to sustain a 7-8-9 relationship. Notice I didn't say *perfect*; I said *expert*. As you become an expert in following the rules and tools, your marital communication culture will be consistently close. Following the rules and tools with exactness will bring you close and keep you close. Let's dissect communication.

SIMPLE COMMUNICATION PATTERN
FOR EVERYONE

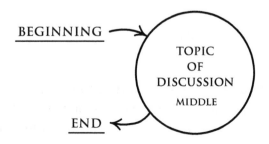

All conversations have a beginning, middle, and end. Each individual in a marriage has their most difficult time in one of these areas. For example, the husband may have a hard time starting any conversation because he is afraid of how his wife will react to the topic (chicken!). The wife may have a hard time discussing a topic because she predicts that her husband will drag it out for two hours, and she doesn't want to ruin the weekend (scaredy-cat!). Both may struggle with ending the conversation because they haven't reached a resolution, and then they feel lousy after spending all that time and energy on a topic that's still not fixed.

In this chapter we will focus on how to begin a conversation. Rule #1, Use Gentle Beginnings, means that every time you start a conversation with your spouse, you should be careful regarding your tone, volume, and attitude.

GENTLE BEGINNINGS

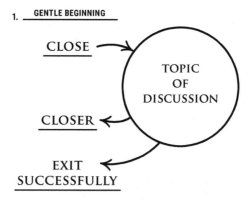

I often ask couples in the first session to explain their communication troubles. This is a common response: "It just starts bad, and we are completely exhausted and angry by the end."

They hate what is happening but continue to misbehave at the onset of every conversation. They are beginning their conversations like 0-5 couples. They are reacting and are living the consequences of having negative assumptions about each other.

One wife in session started a conversation with her husband by saying, "I know you think I'm stupid and can't figure anything out on my own, but believe it or not, I've made a decision, and I want to become a crime scene investigator. Can we talk about how much the schooling will cost?" After this not-so-gentle beginning, the couple never got around to talking about how much the schooling would cost, because they argued for the last ten minutes of the session about whether he thought she was stupid.

When one partner offends their spouse at the onset of a discussion, it generally means they are afraid of that discussion and have already assumed their spouse will be combative and resist what they have to say. When you start a conversation badly, it usually invokes a natural, defensive reaction. How you begin when you talk to your spouse is of utmost importance.

When a conversation begins terribly, it will more than likely end terribly. I've witnessed it thousands of times. When one or both partners begin a conversation with abruptness, rudeness, and disrespect, they are setting themselves up to experience another failure, which brings rapid deterioration. One couple who really did it wrong started most of their conversations with something along these lines: "I AM PISSED. We need to talk right now!" Wow! That's so inviting! Should I press my pants and wear a tie?

Starting a conversation gently seems like an obvious solution to an obvious problem, but this error is one of the most common corrections needed in marriage counseling. It's often the first correction I make with couples, and even after they've been corrected and taught a better way, couples often revert to their previous bad behaviors. They have developed a conditioned response from many bad experiences. It's a part of their marital culture. They haven't recognized that when they begin a conversation negatively, it becomes a major contributor to their dysfunction.

These couples do learn the new rule, however, after they contract and promise to be gentle with each other moving forward. They love the new beginning once they get the feel for it and practice it. Sometimes they are embarrassed and feel a little awkward because it is out of character, kind of Leave-it-to-Beaver like. But many couples have told me, "That was one of the easiest and biggest fixes that changed our relationship for the better."

Another important action that will contribute to a gentle beginning is to recognize the right time to talk. Timing is important. When your spouse is hungry or tired or sick or stressed about something else, it's best to wait for a better time. Both husband and wife need to be prepared and ready at the same time. For example, I may be working on a certain rule or tool in session with a couple. Sometimes the session is scheduled to be about using a certain tool for an issue they need to discuss. But if one or the other person in the room isn't up for it, we work on something else instead.

Timing means each spouse is engaged in the conversation because they are willing and able to talk at that time. Just because an issue is nagging you does not mean it needs to be addressed right now. Even if that issue is bugging you, it's probably not something to dial 911 about. Wait awhile. Try later when you feel it would be better for your spouse. I will address how to invite your spouse to talk later.

Many years ago, when I worked in a drug and alcohol in-patient facility, I learned some tricks to staying clean and sober and preventing relapse. I'm not an addict (unless you count pizza, playing basketball, or watching squirrels and random people and select UFC fights), so I couldn't really relate to some of the patients' struggles with drugs and alcohol. I could relate, however, to something they called H.A.L.T., which stands for Hungry, Angry, Lonely, or Tired. It also means STOP. The idea behind it is that if you are about to relapse, you may not be making a good immediate decision because of these influences on you. The goal is to soothe these influences before indulging in your desired substance. This technique has helped a lot of people to not "fall off the wagon."

Over the years, I came to realize that this quick H.A.L.T. assessment applies to marital communication as well. When a spouse hasn't managed the H.A.L.T. within, they are prone to begin their conversations poorly and to "fall off the wagon" of marital closeness. In your pre-decision to start any conversation gently, assess how you are with H.A.L.T. STOP and manage those symptoms, then proceed when you are calm. Protect the relationship from yourself and your potential misbehavior. Never sacrifice your closeness because of your unchecked H.A.L.T. This tip for success may save you hundreds of hours of regrettable, exhausting conversations.

Here is a quick, brilliant example I use to manage my H.A.L.T.

Hungry: Chico's pizza and Barq's root beer
Angry: Humility and soothing self-talk
Lonely: Serve or call someone
Tired: Sleep or rest (no energy drinks)

Gentle Beginnings Reminder:

You're acting at a 0-5 level at the beginning of a discussion if...

- you are resolution focused.
- you are abrupt and rude.
- your tone and volume are offensive.
- your timing is inappropriate.
- you are assuming the worst about your spouse.
- your spouse shows "allergic" reactions to you
  (wounded, defensive, angry, or shocked).

You're acting at a 7-8-9 level at the beginning of a discussion if...

- you are closeness focused.
- you are gentle and respectful.
- your tone and volume are friendly.
- your timing is decided by your spouse's disposition.
- you are assuming the best about your spouse.
- your spouse shows engaged body language
  (welcoming eye contact, smiling, listening, and supportive).

You have an obligation to welcome and receive your spouse's conversations. As they start conversations gently and the timing is right, be enthusiastic and engaged. 7-8-9 couples don't deny access to talk for no reason.

Healthy, 7-8-9 couples handle issues at frustration level only. They do not wait until they have escalated to agitation or explosion to talk about issues. They are gentle as they begin every conversation. They decide beforehand to be closeness focused, gentle, and calm throughout the conversation. They discipline their actions because they know a 7-8-9 relationship is fragile and must be protected.

7-8-9s are careful with their words because they respect and value their spouse and desire to show it. They want to enjoy their communication and not just get it over with. They are confident that their issues will dissolve as they practice great communication and focus on closeness and love. To reach this outcome, they follow the rules and tools during conversations.

Show your spouse that you are not their enemy, but their friend. Friends enjoy talking to each other; enemies don't.

I recently heard a presidential campaign expert discuss three traits winning candidates have in common: they are positive, uplifting, and forward looking. Without fail, candidates with these traits win elections every time. Similarly, I've found that when individuals show these same qualities when interacting with their spouse, they always win.

⮞ ONE MORE THOUGHT

It's been my pleasure to listen to great people and help them. They have shaped me for the better. I will forever be in their debt. When I first started working as a therapist, people (and their problems) seemed complex, and it was intimidating. However, over the years, I have learned that people want essentially the same thing. They seek therapy because they want some things to stop and other things to start.

Everyone who comes in to therapy is trying to stop thinking or feeling a certain way. They want to stop bad things from happening to them as much as possible, and they want the pain in their life to decrease.

They also want to start having better relationships, more happiness, more peace and joy, and everything else under the sun that makes them feel better. They want to start feeling better and stop feeling so much pain. In therapy, we set goals to make this happen. You don't need therapy to set these goals, but I encourage you to write them down. Your self-change will significantly help with your spouse's happiness and overall well-being.

Stop/Start goals can have a direct, fast, and positive impact on your marriage.

A Stop/Start list might include statements such as these:

- I need to stop bringing up topics late at night and start being aware of my timing.
- I need to stop calling out to you from around the corner and instead start going to where you are and talking face to face.
- I need to stop expecting you to be my alarm clock, and start getting up on my own.

To improve your marriage, stop doing things that cause pain to your spouse, and start doing things that increase pleasure or bring relief for your spouse. That's what 7-8-9 couples do. 0-5 couples don't do this, or they don't do it consistently. They make promises to work on their Stop/Start goals but have poor follow-through.

After you make a Stop/Start list for yourself and about yourself, share it with your spouse. Let them help you clarify it. They'll be happy to teach you how to be a 7-8-9 with them. Have your spouse also make a list, and then give loving and respectful suggestions. Do this in a mature way, then get busy with a consistent effort to make your relationship a close, 7-8-9 relationship. It's the only kind to have. It's the only kind you want.

Chapter 11

Rule #2
Limit Discussions to 2-5 Minutes

"If you can't explain it simply,
 you don't understand it well enough."
                          – Albert Einstein

Despite what you may have learned or assumed about marital communication, you and your spouse should not be talking about a relationship issue for longer than a few minutes in one sitting. Yep, that short. 7-8-9 couples handle each issue a sliver at a time. This means they should have just 2-5 minutes of discussion before they exit the conversation.

THE 2-5 MINUTE LIMIT

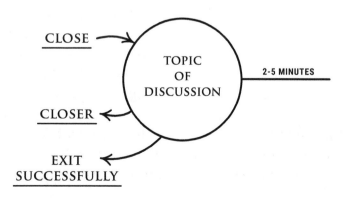

I can tell you right now that either you or your spouse is thrilled about this rule even though I have barely started to explain it. One of you will love the idea that conversations about issues should be short. If that's you, then you're welcome!

When I first tell couples about this essential rule, it's common for either the husband or wife to say, "See, I told you that you talk WAY too long about blah blah blah." If that's the case, you just received a well-deserved therapeutic spanking from your spouse. It's okay. That's part of marriage sometimes.

Years ago, a couple came in for therapy. They had been married for twenty-five years. They struggled to talk about any topic without ending up feeling more distant. When I explained the 2-5 minute rule, the wife looked at her husband and said, "I'll quit glaring at you if you will just follow this one **** rule!" Kind of obvious who the long talker in that marriage was! He figured it out.

This rule may seem impossible at first, but it's a significant rule of 7-8-9 marriages. Couples love it when they realize they can dissolve their issues and sustain their closeness all in one whack. The short time frame keeps couples safe and keeps them from offending each other.

A visual example of the 2-5 minute rule involves ice cream. I tell couples they shouldn't talk about an issue longer than it takes to eat a one-scoop ice cream cone. I've tried it, Baskin Robbins Baseball Nut. The outcome of the brief conversation about more intimacy in our marriage was equally delicious.

If you are the more thorough one, and you are panicking that you can't say everything you need to say and that you won't be heard or understood in that time period, and that you need to give every detail and every example to make your point and talk about everything else that may be associated with how you feel, and everyone you've talked to online agrees with you because they have "liked" your posted comment, and you feel it's a big deal to communicate everything, and you need your spouse to know it's a big deal to communicate everything, and if they don't know it then you can't get your problems resolved with them, and you think that your ice cream cone conversation should be heaped high with all 31 scoops in a gigantic run-on sentence, then you're welcome also. I'm going to help you get the progress and closeness you desire much more effectively and with a lot less work.

Before you start getting any weird ideas about manipulating the 2-5 minute time frame, here are a few suggestions of what *not* to do:

Don't set a timer when you talk.
Don't talk super-fast just to get everything said in the time allotted.
Don't discipline your spouse if they go a little over.

During one session, a husband who was frustrated with his wife constantly reminding him that his time was about up said, "Do you want me nagging you about a time limit when you are talking?" That ended that! Be practical, not rigid. It's a rule, not a commandment.

We've talked about what not to do during these brief conversations; here are some things you *can* do:

Listen and be agreeable and encouraging.
Clarify and get to the specifics of what is being said or asked.
Kindly help your spouse if they are struggling to say what they need.

This problem of overcommunicating is not gender specific. Rather, it's personality and habit driven, so park your gender stereotypes here: _____.

In the past, intimate conversations with your spouse may have been difficult, or the outcome may not have been optimal. Most couples come in to therapy with one or two issues they have repeatedly failed to successfully address. Because they feel stuck, they often feel they *have* to talk longer than 2-5 minutes. However, the idea that more is better is not true in this case, especially when discussing hard topics. Don't do it. You will find that shorter, more frequent conversations will lead to progress.

Before talking about hard issues, you need to be in the right place emotionally, even if you're talking for only 2-5 minutes. I sometimes assign a couple to "find their humility" before we proceed with these hard issues because they are a bit hot or stubborn.

If a husband and wife can find their humility, they will be more likely to be successful. You may want to first have a discussion about how you will find your humility, rather than discussing the topic that's bothering you.

For example, one young husband and wife spent forty-five minutes telling me how their spouse had failed to meet their expectations. After listening, I gave them the assignment to take a week and come prepared to give equal time in session and explain how they personally had fallen short in their marriage and what they were going to do to change it. The next session was profoundly different. When this couple focused on their own imperfections rather than their spouse's imperfections, they found their humility.

Once you've found your humility, each discussion should be navigated carefully and with sincere love. Give your spouse the benefit of the doubt, please.

Some couples have "taboo" topics that they rarely, or never, talk about. Taboo topics include sex, need for affection, conflict between family members, ex-spouses, how many children each wants, finances, whether Lebron James should be MVP every year, and addictive habits. The 2-5 rule works, even with awkward issues.

Following the rules and tools helps any conversation flow like dance steps. An intimate conversation can feel like a slow dance with a stranger. The typical song lasts just a few minutes. Any longer and it starts to feel drawn out and awkward, and the discussion becomes strained. Don't do that to each other. Don't ruin a good thing. Enjoy the time spent, and then go get some donuts and punch. A break from the dance lets you process the experience, marinate on it, and pick up later where you left off. That's enjoyable progress. You'll want to dance with your partner again. Kind of an easy and practical concept, isn't it?

There will be many opportunities to dance with your spouse over the next fifty years. There's no reason to do a marathon dance when discussing your issues. Do your slow dance in the 2-5 minute time frame. There's a lot of wisdom in that sentence. Ponder it. You will see it makes sense.

Years ago, I heard a tip on how to influence a person to like you: "Leave your conversation on a high mark, not a low mark." In other words, don't leave the conversation on a negative or low note. End the conversation when you both are feeling positive and good about what's been said. That person will seek you out again to continue the interaction because the last feeling they had about you was positive, and they want more. Good counsel. Don't you want your spouse to seek you out?

7-8-9 couples keep their communication simple, crisp, and clean. They are effective and productive when they speak about important topics. They know that the longer they talk, the more deterioration can hijack their discussion.

Remember that 0-5 couples are resolution focused, and 7-8-9 couples are closeness focused. 0-5 couples react instead of act. The more they lose their closeness focus and the longer a discussion goes, the greater the chance that the conversation will be complex, confusing, and messy. The more this happens, the more they get lost in deterioration and are swept down the scale of closeness. The rules and tools, followed with exactness, will help protect you from yourself. With no guidelines, a couple risks falling into a pattern of misbehavior. This is not fun.

Another way of looking at the benefit of structured communication is to consider a greeting card message. If a greeting card can express an important message in just seconds, why do you need to talk so long to express everything in your marriage? Yes, I know they're not the same thing, but doesn't a well-edited, well-chosen greeting card send an excellent message in just seconds? I'm giving you 2-5 minutes, for heaven's sake! You really can get your message across with that much time.

Working on an issue briefly leads to progress. Progress gives rise to hope. Hope leads to trust, faith, and closeness. Following the 2-5 minute rule is like eating a slice of cake. I feel much better after eating a slice than I do if I eat the whole cake. Leftovers are a good thing.

Many times in session I hear a great sigh of relief from couples who have successfully learned to use the 2-5 minute rule. They have been trying to get their spouse to talk less and get to the point, or for years they have been avoiding a major issue altogether because they were afraid of a long, drawn-out war. Once they follow the 2-5 minute rule and use the proper tools, they are pleasantly surprised that their message is heard and received much more effectively than an hour-long, evening-long, or marathon conversation about one subject. Long discussions about a topic often feel like nagging. (By the way, the cure to nagging is to speak less.) I believe you will love the 2-5 minute rule once you try it.

By following the 2-5 minute rule and the other rules while discussing your issues, you will be heard and understood with clarity. You will be more liked, loved, wanted, and respected because of that clarity. Your spouse will seek you out to talk because the last time felt great. Your issues will begin to dissolve. At the end of the conversation, you will feel closer to your spouse, instead of being upset and frustrated. You will have more success in a few minutes than if you talked all day.

Earning an Expansion of Time

All that being said, over time, 7-8-9 couples can earn an expansion of time. Expansions of time should be increased in 5-10 minute increments. You earn an expansion of time when you prove to each other that you can follow the rules and tools with exactness and not act out during discussions. This may take a few weeks or months of practice. That's okay. You're not in a hurry. (FYI, if you're taking years to get there, then you need to reread this book together and get serious about your personal change.)

Why do you need an expansion of time? Haven't I been saying it isn't necessary and could be detrimental? Because 7-8-9 couples *want* more time. They have learned that they can transition from one topic to another smoothly because the conversations have become wonderful and friendly. They have changed their marital communication culture to one that is consistent and trustworthy.

Unhealthy couples have few limits on time and follow few or no rules when communicating. Frankly, limits sound dumb to them. They believe it is unnatural to restrict their communication. They continue to try to hammer out issues, or, to preserve peace, they don't talk at all. In the end, without discipline and guidelines, they deteriorate. They are more discouraged at the end of their discussions than when they started. They often experience sudden drops of closeness and spend lots of time making up. They end up taking a walk in the park by themselves and wishing they could have shared that deer sighting with their spouse. It's a lonely outcome. Respect the 2-5 minute rule. I'm helping you make your marital communication easy work so you can enjoy the rest of your time together.

One couple I was seeing had a difficult time following the 2-5 minute rule. After they finally stopped resisting the rule and experienced some success as a result, the wife looked at me and admitted, "It's worth it to stay with it." Yes, it is.

7-8-9 couples don't push extra time on each other. If they both want to talk, they talk. They cooperate and have high awareness of their spouse's desire to talk or not talk. They gently move from one topic to another in an enjoyable way until they desire to do something else. They still manage to progress a sliver at a time and they still dissolve issues, but their biggest gainer is closeness. Their communication culture has changed.

Healthy couples earn the right to determine the length of their communication. They have become experts at the rules and tools and experts on their spouse. The rules and tools have become part of their marital culture. When couples reach this level, that's when I know therapy is about to end. ¡Excelente! They look at me with a smile and say, "I don't think we need to come anymore. We've got this down." Cool stuff.

7-8-9 couples realize it is not healthy to over-talk issues. They make themselves available to each other. They spend the time they had previously wasted on poor communication and use that energy instead for other productive, enjoyable things such as hobbies, talents, socialization, and work. They recognize that talking to each other should be pleasant and gratifying. It feels like walking in the park, holding hands, and having a great time. "Hey look, there's a deer!" That was cool. Hug and kiss.

⤳ ONE MORE THOUGHT

0-5 marriages are marriages of inaction. These couples semi-commit and procrastinate. They make grand promises but don't deliver. One client told her husband in session, "I don't care what you *say* anymore. I only care what you *do* from now on." I thought to myself, "Atta girl."

Being married to a partner who is not fully committed is exhausting. Over time, the disappointed spouse lowers their expectations just to survive the relationship. The offending spouse causes their partner to guess what's going on, to wonder if things will ever get better, and to beg for the things they need. They don't recognize or don't care that they are toying with the most important relationship in their life. Their energies are focused on themselves, not their spouse. If that's you, you can do better.

7-8-9 marriages are marriages of action. When 7-8-9 couples say they are going to do something, they do it. After a 2-5 minute discussion about a change their spouse would like them to make, 7-8-9s get busy. They like to be taught what to do, and they don't need constant supervision. They are proactive and do their best, right away, to show their spouse they are invested in the permanent changes their spouse has asked of them.

7-8-9 couples don't "forget." They don't rationalize their failure to change. When they make mistakes, they take responsibility for them. They follow up with their spouse to see if the changes they were asked to make are acceptable, or if improvements are needed. The changes they are making are not just for their spouse, but for themselves.

They want to be the best they can for their spouse. They are eager to make their spouse happy and do not want to cause their spouse pain. Understandably, they would like these actions and feelings to be reciprocated. Each spouse's energy is focused not on himself or herself but on both of them as a couple. If that's you, well done.

Chapter 12

Rule #3
End Your Linking

"Halfway through any work, one is often tempted to go off on a tangent. Once you have yielded, you will be tempted to yield again and again..."

– Barbara Hepworth

The biggest contributor to communication clutter in marriage is linking. Linking is when a couple begins a conversation with one subject in mind, but then ends up linking multiple issues to it.

END YOUR LINKING

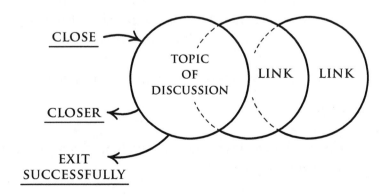

95

You probably made paper link chains in grade school. It was fun, and the longer you made the chain, the better you felt. Linking issues when you communicate is like that, except that making your conversations longer doesn't make you feel better.

Linking also involves getting off subject or getting distracted during a conversation. Linking happens for three reasons:

1. A couple is resolution focused and believes they need to accomplish all they can in one sitting to be productive. The couple adds other topics to the conversation because they are loosely or directly related to the issue being discussed. They think that since they are related in some way, they need to be discussed at that time. They don't.

2. The couple has been bottling up multiple issues because they have been avoiding, or are scared of, conflict. When they can't handle the agitation any longer, they feel the need to "get it all out."

3. It's a habit that one or the other brought into the relationship from a prior relationship or from their family of origin.

Most couples don't even recognize they are linking, and that it is problematic, until I bring it to their attention. When it is explained to them, they are relieved that they can stop it. It's been a burden to them and the relationship. Linking issues together rarely has a happy ending. Linking sounds like this:

Kevin: "Ashley, I'd like to talk to you about the checkbook."

Ashley: "Sure."

Kevin: "Will you leave the checkbook next to my backpack when you are done with it, please?"

Ashley: "I can do that."

Kevin: "Because last week I wanted to order a pizza and I couldn't find it. You know, I can't seem to find quite a few things that you misplace."

Ashley: "I do? Like what?"

Kevin: "A lot of things. It seems you are really like your mother in how forgetful she is. Just the other day she forgot to pick up the kids, remember?"

Ashley: "Well, I don't think it was exactly like that, but..."
Kevin: "I really don't think she should be watching our kids anymore. Do you agree?"

Ashley: "Well, I don't know about that either."

Kevin: "You know, whenever we are talking, you say, 'I don't know' too much. Do you really not know, or are you just saying that? Kind of like how you told me that we should go camping last summer. Then you told me you didn't know if you wanted to go. You seem to have a hard time committing to things. We need to talk about that as well and about you leaving your curling iron on all day. I don't want the house catching on fire. Can we start with those things?"

Ashley: "I guess. Can I go take some Excedrin first?"

I find that there is a dominant "linker" in most relationships. In the first session with a couple, the therapist quickly figures out who the linker is because they are the most irritating person in the room. I know that sounds rude, but it's true. I frequently and politely tell them to say more with fewer words. It's hard for them at first, but they can be trained. Not many people want to be the most irritating one in the room.

I have had spouses say to me, "Thank you for catching that. For some reason, he (or she) can't hear me when I tell him (or her) that." It's probably because the person is trying to figure out what they are about to link next.

If a couple has a problem talking about just one subject successfully, then doesn't it stand to reason that they will struggle when talking about multiple problems, one right after the other?

When a couple has a problem that needs to be addressed, they need to discuss that problem without additional clutter. Linking is not just a bad habit; it is a dysfunctional pattern that frustrates couples and makes communication complex, confusing, and messy. It causes fatigue in relationship closeness.

7-8-9 couples always seek simple, crisp, and clean technique. They love enjoyable conversations. They handle one issue at a time. Unhealthy couples treat their communication like a Rubik's cube, with lots of random twists and turns. Healthy couples simply take the stickers off of the Rubik's cube and color code each side with exactness. Yes, they cheat and make communication simple so the outcome is successful. Neither spouse minds that.

7-8-9s know life's problems don't require difficult communication techniques. They want to feel closer, not more distant, at the end of the conversation. They are disciplined in how they talk to each other. They want to save their time and energy on simply enjoying each other while they talk. They're always on the same team.

⇗ ONE MORE THOUGHT

I don't like crabgrass, so every time I mow the lawn, I scour my yard to get rid of that noxious weed. One day I pulled a patch of that wicked weed and realized I had none left to pull. I kept looking, just to make sure. It was true. It was all gone. I stood there for a moment and thought, "Now what?" Then I realized I could just enjoy the grass.

When couples pull the last noxious weed — in this case, linking — from their communication, they begin talking with greater clarity. Their communication becomes more efficient and simple. Now it's as if they are unsure what to do with their newfound time. Weeding out bad habits from your communication feels great. Just enjoy it.

Chapter 13

Rule #4
Edit What You Say

*"You are much more attractive
when you edit what you say."*
– Glade Daniels-Brown

Perhaps the most important rule that helps couples stay out of hot water is the art of editing. If I could give someone only one piece of marital advice, it would be to edit what you say.

One man told me he had made a "fatal error" when communicating with his wife on their honeymoon. As a young man, he was under the false assumption that, because he was married, he could openly and directly say what he was thinking and feeling as long as it was respectful. "She is my best friend, so..."

While on their honeymoon, his wife asked him how she looked in her new lingerie. He said that she looked a little chubby, but was still hot. She turned right around and went back into the bathroom. After some coaxing, she came out with a hotel robe on, and that was the end of that evening. He laughed as he told me the story and admitted, "I'm still paying a huge price for that one word." Fifteen years later, he's still dealing with the fallout in their sexual life.

"Chubby" is funny when you're talking to your best guy friend and he asks how he looks before he heads out on a blind date. However, editing "chubby" from this man's communication with his wife would have been wise, not only for that night, but for decades to come. That husband learned that not everything needs to be said.

One woman I saw in therapy had experienced a lot of conflict with her spouse over the years. She struggled with editing also. She was big-time into horses, and her husband was doing his best to buy the right gift for her. She had previously complained that her husband never thought of her on holidays and special occasions. I visited with the husband a few times and encouraged him to change this to improve his marriage. He made the commitment to change.

Weeks before her birthday, he put a lot of thought into her present, and he ended up buying her the nicest saddle he could afford. He even had it custom sized for her horse. Pleased with his efforts, he presented it to her on her birthday. He really wanted his wife to be happy. What he didn't know is that she was expecting something more along the lines of jewelry or cruise tickets.

When she opened the present, she was visibly upset, and she said to him, "You bought me a saddle for my (bleeping) birthday? Do I look like a (bleeping) horse?" As could be expected, he was pretty hesitant to get her a surprise of any kind after being bucked off like that.

It's hard to say everything the right way all the time, but it is possible to say things better most of the time.

Unhealthy couples' unedited communication could be compared to a man walking into a room with a ten-pound bag of flour, cutting the end open, and whipping it around the room everywhere. It's reckless. It's messy. The couple ends up cleaning up that mess for days, weeks, months, and sometimes years. Words that sting and degrade need deep cleaning many times over in a relationship.

Of course, these couples need to work on other issues, such as forgiveness, forgetting, and moving forward. But the reality is, editing what you say is going to save you a lot of work and prevent the need to spend years trying to heal.

Back to the flour analogy. Healthy, 7-8-9 couples take that same ten-pound bag of flour, cut open the end, carefully pour it into a canister, and then measure out what they need to make a delicious dessert. They are careful and precise in how they talk. They're not paranoid in how they say things; they are just considerate, loving, and charitable.

But isn't editing kind of like lying? No. Lying is self-interested; those who lie do so in an attempt to protect themselves. Editing is not self-interested; it is simply an attempt to be protective of someone else while also being honest. Yes, it is possible to lie while you are editing, but I'm not condoning that. Editing is being protective of the other person and of the closeness of the relationship. It's being kind, nice, and respectful while still telling the truth that is necessary for the situation.

For example, I watched a young married couple edit themselves very nicely during a session. A few years back, when they had been talking about each other's parents, the husband said, "I think you know that your mom is not my favorite person to spend more than two or three days with." She replied, "In all honesty, two or three days with us is probably ideal for her also."

Unedited, the husband's statement would have sounded like this: "I think you know I can't deal with your mom, and after two or three days, she pushes me toward Insane-ville." The wife could have responded, "Well, after two or three days, you drive my mom to consider a restraining order."

Can you imagine if you were like Garfield the cat, with your every thought broadcast in thought bubbles above your head? Everyone could see everything you were thinking, and you could see everything everyone else was thinking. I think that would be awful. I believe people are generally good, but if every thought was transparent and unedited, we would have a world war with no survivors. Luckily, we aren't like Garfield. From our thought bubble to our mouth, we must edit to avert war.

There are two types of communication editing. Some individuals under-edit what they say, like that thought bubble. They believe they are entitled to say anything. I've heard men and women in session say, "I should be able to say whatever is on my mind, and my spouse should be able to handle it." This is reckless and is asking for serious trouble. Under-editors say too much and offend frequently.

Over-editors say almost nothing at all and leave their spouse to fill in the blanks or to make assumptions. One client told me, "My spouse won't talk. I ask a question when we are in the car, and ten miles go by without any answer, or I get an 'I don't know.'" Over-editing, like under-editing, is unhealthy and creates distance between spouses.

So, we have under-editing and over-editing. What is the right amount of editing in a marriage? The right amount of editing is saying what you need to say while sustaining a 7-8-9 level of closeness, without lying.

Editing is a rule. It is crucial to follow this rule and develop this skill if you want to have a close, 7-8-9 marriage. You will love that your spouse edits when speaking to you.

Chapter 14

Rule #5
Slow down

*"Order marches with weighty
and measured strides.
Disorder is always in a hurry."*
– Napoleon Bonaparte

W hen I am driving and come upon a reduced speed zone, my natural tendency is to disobey it. I feel annoyed that I have to slow down. I like to speed. I don't like the restrictions that speed limits place on me. I want to go faster than the limit without consequences. That's just me.

Most of the time there is a reason for speed reductions. Maybe it's a pedestrian area or school zone. The protection of others and the protection of oneself is the reason behind the reduction. With the benefit of hindsight, I've looked back on my life and thought, "If only I'd obeyed that one rule, I wouldn't be dealing with this right now." I'm probably not alone in this.

In marital communication, these safety measures are called rules. The rules in this book will provide protection for you and your spouse. Happy couples follow these rules, even if they want to resist them. Unhappy couples feel they are an exception and need no restrictions.

When I see a couple resist rules in session and simply tolerate them without internalizing them, I know they are at high risk of deterioration and backsliding. One husband I met with in session refused to follow the rules of communication. He told me, "I'm different from most people. I just want to lay all the facts out on the table and quit beating around the bush with all this nonsense." His wife remained quiet. This couple lasted only a few sessions, because the husband resisted the rules. They came in to their first session as a 1 on the closeness scale and left their third session as a 1. That's not the kind of outcome I was hoping for.

When couples resist rules, after a few months or years, I see these couples again, and they are in an even worse spot than the first time I saw them. Why do that to your relationship and yourself? Your time with each other is too valuable. 7-8-9 couples don't risk damaging the most important relationship they have simply because they want to act impulsively.

Like speed limits slow down vehicles on the road, happy couples literally slow down their speech when they communicate. They use personal discipline and follow the rule of slowing down, even if their instincts are telling them to speed up. The more important the topic, the more they should slow down. They know that if they slow down, they can be careful and edit as they go; they can be precise and accurate. Their spouse will understand them with more clarity.

7-8-9s know that if they speed through a topic, they are at risk of making significant errors. They know that even if an issue feels like an emergency, it's not really an emergency.

Happy couples decide beforehand that their discussion will be successful. Just as a careful driver makes adjustments to changing circumstances in traffic, so do 7-8-9s as they communicate. They are always adjusting and attempting to make the ride of communication pleasant. As they travel through an issue together, the real goal of their communication is to be closer at the end of the ride than they were at the beginning.

Bad drivers are a menace to everyone on the road. They want to do what they want to do, and they don't really care about anyone around them. They believe everyone should adjust to them, not the other way around. They cause wrecks and injure others.

Unhappy couples behave and communicate with the same reasoning as bad drivers. They speed up when they talk. They let their emotions dictate their conversation. They recklessly fly through issues in an effort to resolve them, thinking that this will allow them to get what they want and therefore be happier with each other. By speeding up, they feel they are being more productive. They feel they are more in control and that they have the upper hand in the debate.

Unhappy couples act as if every issue is an emergency that needs to be addressed quickly to make the pain go away. In their hurry, they inadvertently increase their own and their spouse's pain, and they make future communication even more complex, confusing, and messy. In the end, they are more distant from their spouse than when they started. And now they have to repair all the damage they have caused by speeding up and rolling and crashing like an out-of-control NASCAR wreck.

One couple I saw struggled mightily with speeding up whenever they discussed an issue. They were highly defensive and quick to respond to each other. The wife was prone to swearing when upset. The more upsetting the topic, the quicker the conversation went. The quicker the conversation went, the more she would get upset. The more she would get upset, the more she would swear.

After one such discussion, I interrupted her to ask where she had learned to swear so much. She said, "I learned to swear like a sailor because my dad was an (F-ing) sailor!" When we don't manage the discussion, it manages us, eliciting raw emotion and dredging up bad habits.

Let's briefly talk golf. Even though you can hack your way to the green by slamming the ball with a wood driver, making a three-foot putt should be done with careful consideration. When you discuss an important issue with your spouse, be exact and use a careful, smooth stroke so you can finish well.

Chapter 15
_____

Rule #6
Only Discuss Issues When You're "Off Hot"

"The greatest remedy for anger is delay."
– Thomas Paine

A s a young man, I had the opportunity to pick rocks from a farmer's field all day in plus ninety-degree weather without any shade. It was grueling. I remember thinking, "This is the worst job in the world." I also remember believing that if we picked all the rocks we could see from the field, our job would be done. At the end of the day, it felt good to see hundreds of rocks on the flatbed truck. I even recognized many of the larger boulders and remembered the pain of lifting them. As I sat with my friends later that day and ate hamburgers and drank root beer, we felt accomplished in our exhaustion. To this day, that was the best-tasting meal of my life. That day bonded us as friends, gave us a great story to tell, and taught us respect for honest labor.

Then I learned something that ruined the moment. The farmer overheard us talking about being finished with picking all the rocks in the field, and he said with a smile, "Oh, we're not done. New rocks will surface." At that moment I was really mad. I was hot with anger. What a waste of a full day!

"What are you talking about?" we asked. He explained that large rocks vibrate to the top as smaller rocks settle under them and push them up. I remember being disappointed that all our work was for nothing. Why were we doing all this if more rocks would surface later? It seemed a hopeless endeavor.

The farmer reassured us that it wasn't hopeless. He taught us that if we were consistent in picking the rocks, the larger ones would eventually disappear, and the smaller ones would be much more manageable and workable. He taught us that this kind of work was done in steps and that the field was better because of the work we had done. He let us know that the smaller rocks would be fine in the dirt and he could still have an excellent crop. They didn't all have to be removed as we previously thought. After hearing this, we were less upset.

Issues in marriage are like those rocks in the field. Even if you pick the large rocks on top and remove them, more will surface. Don't be discouraged about this. It is normal in all marriages. As you are patient in managing the large issues successfully, the issues become smaller and smaller over time until they can coexist with your closeness.

This is why unhappy couples fail when they are resolution focused and not closeness focused. They believe that issues need to be quickly and completely removed for the crop of closeness to grow. They are hot about their issues most of the time, and they make the mistake of discussing them when they are hot.

A funny young married couple I saw in session illustrates why "off hot" is a rule. The wife learned from her mother that "You have to be angry at men in order to be heard." Her poor husband was as gentle-hearted as a sloth. All he needed was eye contact and a little love, and he would give his wife all he had. When she learned to stop going after him like a Marine in battle and act more like a kind zoo staff member, giving him some fruit or a leaf to chew on while patting him on the head, things went much more smoothly.

7-8-9 couples know that the goal is closeness, not resolution. They know that their issues can improve step by step, over time, and while they are working toward that, they still enjoy their closeness. As a result, they're able to relax and discuss their issues when they are "off hot." In other words, they wait until they can discuss things without getting fired up about it. They know that emotions cause them to react and act inappropriately, so they manage their emotions rather than letting their emotions manage them. They act rather than react when they speak. They protect their relationship from themselves and their tempers.

One couple who seemed to communicate quite well came in to counseling. But it soon became apparent that sometimes their communication would quickly turn hot. Luckily, they would cool down fairly quickly, so that was a plus. They laughed that their communication was like a Jack-in-the-box. The music would be playing nicely as they turned their communication crank, and then suddenly that ugly, weird clown would jump out and startle both of them. They were almost shocked by the ending they created.

Even though a couple may start with a gentle beginning, the "hot" part can appear suddenly and without much warning. Over the years, I have observed that this shift from peaceful discussion to ugly, weird clown happens when a couple shifts from closeness focus to resolution focus. As this couple changed their focus to one of closeness and applied a few rules (editing, not linking, and only discussing issues when off hot), they were able to shove the clown into the box, tape it shut, and just enjoy the music.

I love playing basketball. I think it's the greatest sport ever, and I hope to play until I'm at least sixty. However, after I play, I end up with inflammation. I eventually learned to take a cool bath or shower to reduce that inflammation so I could play another day. I also learned that professional athletes take an ice bath or use a cryogenic chamber to help them recover. That's the quick way to recovery.

All couples need to take a type of ice bath before they have a conversation. They need to start and finish their conversations cool and prevent unreasonable "inflammation" as they talk. Happy couples try to start cool and end cool. Never head into an issue hot. Cool yourself and come prepared to be closer to your spouse instead of focusing on resolving the upsetting issue. To cool yourself means you come back to talk after you mentally prepare yourself to enthusiastically follow the rules and tools.

Chapter 16

Rule #7
Allow Restarts

Mulligan:
An extra stroke, not counted on the scorecard,
allowed after a poor shot in informal golf

A ll couples make mistakes when they communicate. Throughout your marriage, you and your spouse will inevitably
mess up when you start talking about something, even
when you're doing your best to edit your words and be respectful. Expect it from yourself. Expect it from your spouse. When it
happens, neither of you is going to like what's been said, so it's
important to allow a restart or mulligan, or in other words, to
give your spouse a second chance. Have you ever made one of
these mistakes and then said, "What I meant to say was...", but
then your spouse didn't really let the first thing go? The restart
rule ensures that the last thing that was said is let go and that
you are given a chance to restate what you really meant.

One couple told me about a commitment the husband had
made early in their relationship in the stupidity of love. He had
said, "I'll give you a foot massage whenever you need one."

Years later, she would be in the back bedroom expecting a foot massage while he sat in the living room watching T.V. after a hard day's work. He knew what she wanted from many prior observations, and he did his best to avoid his regretted contract. She would remind him of his earlier promise by simply yelling, "You said!" In some situations, such as these, restarts can be allowed years later.

7-8-9 couples charitably give their spouse a second chance to say things right when they talk. They know that when they are discussing important topics, communication can be confusing and messy. Emotions and feelings are difficult to express. When I make a mistake, or when what I am saying seems to be going in the wrong direction, I simply say, "I need to restart," without being punished for doing so. I need to have that merciful gift given to me. If it is, I am merciful in return. Hey, even runners and swimmers are allowed a restart if they make a mistake off the block. Shouldn't intimate communication in marriage be allowed a restart?

Unhappy couples are typically unforgiving of their spouse's errors. They remember their spouse's words and use them as leverage against each other in future conversations. I call this "lawyering" because of the next story. Lawyering turns a couple's communication into Right vs. Wrong arguments. It causes each spouse to be defensive. However, 7-8-9s are not on trial.

A really sharp couple I worked with learned to love restarts. Both lawyers with Type A personalities, they were fairly blunt when they talked. However, they were still humans with feelings, so being blunt caused them deterioration in their closeness. They felt pretty low on the scale, around a level 4, during one session. The husband looked at his wife and said in frustration, "You know, marriage sucks!" (That's when the fight started.)

She started crying and said, "Well, you know, I sometimes hate you, too."

He quickly said, "Wait, I need to restart. What I meant to say is that I hate being a 3 or 4 with you. I want to be in the 7-8-9 range with you, and marriage sucks when we are so low in our numbers."

She allowed the restart and then did a little cleanup of her own for the hate comment. You see, husbands and wives become their best selves when their spouse shows some common-sense courtesy.

I've listened to hundreds of conversations between husbands and wives where restarts could and should have been implemented. I've often thought to myself, "Man, I'll bet you wish you could take that back right now."

When a couple doesn't restart, or allow a restart, the contention and communication clutter escalates quickly. A whole session could be consumed with back-and-forth defenses and arguments. The damage of those words can last a lifetime. As a marital therapist, these are the worst sessions. I attempt to stop the carnage several times, but sometimes it's to no avail. Sometimes people pay to fight in front of me. I sometimes surrender, make a bowl of popcorn, and start imagining how I will poke around my garage or organize my tools over the weekend. What a waste of a session.

Here's another situation where a restart should have been allowed but wasn't. I experienced this firsthand.

A young man in college was walking hand in hand with his girlfriend. They had been dating for about two months and were going out to dinner to start a great weekend. As they headed to his truck in the parking lot of his apartment complex, they were in the 10 zone of closeness. In a wonderful open moment of flirtatious trolling, the girlfriend asked the young man, "What made you want to ask me out in the first place?"

In his ignorance, he thought he could say whatever he was thinking. He replied, "Well, actually I was going to ask your roommate Ashley out, but she wasn't home at the time."

The girlfriend unlocked her fingers from his, kicked his truck tire, and walked away, never to be seen again. Never was there a better time for a restart or the receiving of a restart. Yep, that was me.

Now, had I been given the opportunity to have a restart, I would have said, "Wait. What I meant to say was, I'm glad she wasn't home, because then I got the chance to ask you out. I didn't think I would have a chance with you, so I was going to settle for her. It all worked to my advantage. I'm sorry that came out wrong. I'm not so good at presenting things." Life-altering trauma avoided.

When your spouse needs a restart, let go of the last words they said, and allow a new beginning, without inflicting a consequence for what was said or how it was said. This allows for clean, efficient communication without causing unnecessary debates or arguments. Happy couples assume the best about their spouse. Unhappy couples assume the worst. Please assume that your spouse wants a 7-8-9 relationship with you, and realize they will make mistakes in the communication process. Allowing mistakes and letting them go is essential to 7-8-9 communication.

If you will follow this rule and allow restarts, you will feel relieved and happier. You will feel better that your spouse is self-correcting. In return, you will appreciate being given the latitude to make errors and not be punished for them. 7-8-9 couples don't get bent out of shape with their spouse's communication errors. Instead, they smile and quickly give them a pass, knowing that the same kindness will be extended to them when it is their turn to talk.

I promise that as you are quick to let go and quick to forgive, and as you encourage your spouse when he or she errs, both of you will feel even closer at that moment than you did five seconds earlier. Test it.

7 RULES

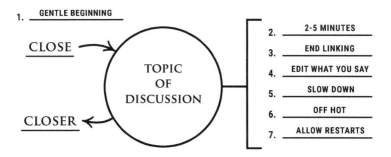

Chapter 17

Teach and Train Vs. Guess, Wonder, and Beg

"Tell me and I forget.
Teach me and I remember.
Involve me and I learn."
– Benjamin Franklin

Now that we've finished discussing the 7 rules of marital communication, we're ready to move on to the 3 tools used by spouses in 7-8-9 marriages. But first we need to talk about a couple of things.

The funny thing about marriage relationships is that often, couples believe that after being married a certain amount of time, their spouse can, or should, be able to read their mind. This, of course, is completely ridiculous. Yes, you may at times guess correctly what the other person is thinking, but relying on mind reading as a communication strategy is not a good idea.

Couples who expect their spouse to read their mind or know exactly what they are thinking end up being disappointed. They become angry and resentful and say things like, "You should know by now that I want to be treated like this," or "I can't believe you don't get it. You must not care." A favorite statement of mine, one that is often repeated in session, is this: "If you loved me, you would have figured it out by now." These kinds of comments hinder future efforts to "figure it out" and lessen your spouse's desire to try.

Unhealthy couples keep their spouse guessing and wondering what they are thinking, and they make them beg for change and attention. Making your spouse guess, wonder, and beg is disrespectful to the marital covenant. It is not loving or caring. Continuing these behaviors will cause significant deterioration and keep couples below a 5 on the scale of closeness.

0-5 couples often believe that their spouse—to show they care—should have to work hard to understand them. They believe their spouse needs to be tested or tricked into making desired changes because they don't believe their spouse will deliver when given simple requests. This need for trickery comes from failed previous attempts to get what they needed legitimately. As a result of these failures, they give up or quit trying so hard. Instead, they come up with ways to bypass simple requests and use manipulation to get their needs and wants met.

For example, one couple came to see me because they felt a lack of closeness in their marriage. During one session, the wife asked her husband why they had to go to the movies so often on their dates. He paused for a second and then looked at me and said, "I want to go to the movie theater with her so she won't be getting up and doing the laundry and dishes like she does at home every time we watch a movie. I just want her to sit next to me."

I asked him if he had told his wife why he wanted her to sit next to him, and he said, "No, it would sound too corny."

I suggested that he tell her right then why it was important to him, even if he thought it was corny. So he told her. She thought his reason for wanting her to sit by him was sweet. The likelihood of her changing that behavior was far greater because now she understood what movies were actually about to him. His trick had little to do with movies and a lot to do with feeling emotionally distant from his wife.

Instead of relying on tricks or expecting their spouse to read their mind, 7-8-9 couples respect each other by doing something different. With exactness and simplicity, they teach and train each other what they need and want. They clearly explain what will work for them. In doing so, they are respectful and never controlling. The reward for all that training is a very good partner.

Unhappy couples view teaching and training as condescending or controlling. It is not. 7-8-9s love to be taught and trained because it is a quick and efficient way to find out what their spouse needs and wants. 7-8-9s know that exactness leads to closeness.

If you expect to be a 7-8-9, you need to be trainable. This requires you to humble yourself, drop your defenses, and open your heart. It requires self-discipline and an enthusiastic effort to progress. It means controlling the urges and passions that get in the way of closeness. It requires a selfless inner change and a desire to have integrity. A 7-8-9 is earned. Earning a 7-8-9 means you are sincerely seeking to know your spouse so you know how to help their life run smoothly and have a 7-8-9 with you.

A mechanic came in to a session with his wife. They were in big trouble with their marriage. He had all but given up on understanding her. After we discussed the principle of teaching and training, he quickly got it. He said, "I can go online and get the manual for the make and model of any car and know what to do to fix it. I guess what you are saying is that I need to go to her [pointing to his wife], and she can tell me exactly what will fix her? Hey, that's better than a manual!" Uh huh.

We then began to discuss the tools he could use to help him "fix her." I knew he would like the concept of using tools to fix things. Once your spouse has given you the manual of how they work, continue to work on those things that they have taught you. Lather, rinse, repeat, day after day, week after week. One way 7-8-9s teach and train is in the form of a Request for Change or Information. This is explained in chapter 19.

I sort of like the movie *The Wizard of Oz*. It is packed with marital hints. For example, do you remember when Dorothy and the Scarecrow find the Tin Man? Can you imagine what would have happened if they had just given up on him and walked away because they didn't know what he was moaning about? Instead of just leaving him there, they work to understand just enough from him to oil his mouth. The Tin Man feels relief and exclaims, "My goodness! I can talk again!" He then teaches and trains Dorothy and the Scarecrow exactly where to apply more oil to help him.

When you allow your spouse to teach you, listen and follow their direction. They know what they need and want. They will help you know what they need and want. Simple teaching and training will lead to better results.

I often hear that teaching and training one's spouse can feel a bit awkward. It probably will be. Do it anyway. All intimate gains in marriage are awkward, but we don't stop making intimate efforts just because they are awkward. To have a 7-8-9 marriage, you must take courageous risks in your relationship.

Chapter 18

Healthy Marriages Use Tools

*"If you ever are in your everyday life,
and you feel like you just accomplished something big
that you had going on, then that's Beast Mode.
It's an accomplishment that you put yourself through something
to get something better out of it. I feel that's Beast Mode."*

— Marshawn Lynch

I learn so much from the couples I work with. They teach me and selflessly distribute marital wisdom and insights during every session. They say a lot of funny things such as, "Okay! I'm only giving you One More Last Chance!"

One wife said to her husband, "My emotions are not enjoying your company." Another wife, when asked by her husband what they needed to change in their marriage, exclaimed, "What do we need to change!? The only thing we need to change is everything!"

Couples tell a lot of funny stories about the frustrations of living with another person. I asked one couple if they were dating weekly. The wife answered, "Oh yeah, we date all right. We drive through a fast food place, and my husband counts that as a date. Sometimes the entertainment is eating the burger in the car as we sit through the automatic car wash and watch the friggin' bubbles!"

These couples share valuable things they have figured out along the way. "We have a BTA relationship. Better than alone," one husband confided. Another said, "I've learned it is much easier to forgive and forget than to remember and hate."

To keep communication running like a well-oiled machine, couples must employ the four P's: Practice Positive Predictable Patterns. Practicing positive predictable patterns in marriage keeps the partners in a marriage feeling close. It is similar to anything we practice in life. The more we practice correctly, the better the experience. Sports are a simple example of this.

When I play basketball, I'm reminded why it's the best sport on the planet. It's just fun. Well, it is unless guys who don't understand the game show up. When I am on defense and am guarding my opponent, someone from the opposing team could "screen" me (prevent me from guarding my opponent). This would force me to go around the screen and get back to my opponent and continue to guard him. If my teammates don't tell me that a screen is happening on my left or right side, I run into the screen/person, and it hurts. It is also annoying and frustrating, especially when the guy I am supposed to be guarding makes the open shot.

In marriage, to prevent both spouses from being injured, each partner must communicate with the other about "screens," or situations, as they come. Life moves quickly. When a couple cooperates and practices positive predictable patterns together (using tools and rules such as editing what you say and allowing restarts), they can maneuver around obstacles with the least amount of damage possible. They feel safe. When couples feel safe, they can allow themselves to be vulnerable while discussing intimate subjects.

To improve their marriage, 7-8-9s follow simple rules and use specific, reliable tools. There are really only three tools necessary to have a 7-8-9 relationship. These tools, discussed in the next few chapters, need to be learned, practiced, and applied regularly, or they will be neglected or forgotten. As you face obstacles in your marriage, refer to these chapters for a refresher. Regular use of the rules and tools will change the culture of your relationship and help you know what to do when you are faced with problems. The tools will allow you to clean up errors, address needed changes, and connect deeply with your spouse. Using all three tools will help you keep your 7-8-9 intact.

7-8-9s closely follow the rules and tools when they talk about difficult subjects. If they are a little nervous or unsure as to how to proceed, they follow the script, and it guides them through the process. Most people cannot remember everything they have learned from dozens of books about marriage. They suffer from information overload and don't need more clutter. They need a simple script instead. Once they have a good understanding of the tools, they can use the scripts of "Request for Change" and "Cleanups" to help them discuss important matters.

I have found that a simple, trustworthy set of rules and tools is necessary for couples to be successful. It's step-by-step work. One wife explained to me, "I did one thing right, and he did one thing right, and then good stuff started to happen."

We developed a model for communication because our goal is to help couples simplify their communication. Even more importantly, we developed this model because we want couples to experience consistent 7-8-9 closeness. A 0-5 marriage is unfulfilling, and besides that, it's just too much work.

Years ago, I worked with an amazing couple. After learning about the 0-10 scale of closeness, the husband said something awesome to his wife. He was a 6 on the scale, and his wife said she was a 5. They had been in a roommate relationship for years. He looked at his wife and said, "I didn't choose you because I wanted to have a 5 or 6 marriage. I could have chosen anyone to have a 5-6 with. I chose you because I wanted a 9 marriage, and I believed you wanted the same."

It turns out that the wife did want the same thing her husband did. They completed their sessions with a solid 7-8-9, and off they went. It's important for couples to remind each other what they wanted in the beginning and where they want to be now. If this doesn't happen, apathy will become the norm.

Some couples I have worked with remind me of a story I read years ago. A mother and daughter got lost in a large corn maze around Halloween. The corn maze shut down at closing time and the staff left for the night. The mother and daughter were accidentally left alone in the maze. They tried for hours to find their way out. They were getting cold and scared. The mother called 911, and help eventually arrived. I found this incident kind of funny, but at the same time, I could understand their panic. Having lived around corn fields my whole life, I was surprised that the mother didn't just follow a row of corn until it led her out to a ditch or road. Instead, she kept wandering around in the maze. In marriage, wandering around in confusing communication will leave you lost, frustrated, and disoriented. You may feel as if the problem is turning into a 911 situation. Following the simple rows of rules and tools while talking about important things will help you get out of that lost, frustrated feeling.

Decide beforehand to use the rules and tools before every conversation. Walking into discussions just hoping that everything will go well is what 0-5s do. 7-8-9s decide ahead of time to make great interactions happen with disciplined communication.

At the beginning of my sessions with couples, I promise them that if they will follow the rules and tools with exactness, they will complete sessions as a 7-8-9 couple. I promise that if you are consistent with these simple rules and tools, you will sustain your 7-8-9 for life. I love watching couples succeed after they've unsuccessfully tried other methods to improve their marriage. After using the rules and tools for just a few weeks, they have renewed hope. I frequently hear, "Our relationship is better now than it has ever been," and "This seems too simple to work this quickly and easily, yet it does if we just follow the script." And lastly, I hear, "This would be incredible if we could be like this forever." I remind all couples that it is up to them to follow the rules and tools daily, and if they do so, they will continue to be a solid 7-8-9. Only selfishness, pride, and lack of desire can stop a couple from having this type of experience.

Tools help you and your spouse see your faults and commit to change. They allow you to become someone or something greater than you were before. When you become your best self, your marriage will become greater. Without this internal change, your chances of a 7-8-9 relationship will decrease.

A 7-8-9 marriage requires both of you to be your best self. The work is worth the payoff. Your focus should be on self-improvement and closeness, not on spousal change. That will come. Your diligent self-work will be the example and motivation for your spouse to change.

How do you make these changes? Set daily goals and make them a pattern. Stick with them. When you increase your integrity, you will like yourself more. As you change, your spouse will find you more attractive and will seek you out. The good changes you make will make other changes more desirable. They will also make the bad behaviors less appealing.

One good man I worked with finally quit drinking after 30 years. After conquering his drinking problem, this man was then motivated to shave daily and lose weight. As a result, his wife found a renewed attraction to him, and he never wanted to go back to the way he was before.

⤷ ONE MORE THOUGHT

You are great. With that knowledge, your marriage will become great. Pull yourself out of hibernation, dormancy, and apathy by choosing to wake up and improve. Encourage yourself upward. Help your spouse aim high. Let them know what you see in them. When you build their self-confidence, you will end up with an even better spouse. You're going to like the outcome. On to the tools!

Chapter 19

Tool #1
Request for Change or Information

"You're never too good to get better.
Take that and apply it to everything in your life."
                                    – Benson Henderson

C ountless times, I have heard a false statement about change in marriage. The statement is this: "You shouldn't try to change your spouse."

Although an individual's personality is fairly immovable, this statement is still false. The reality is, you will need your spouse to change many things. They will do things that frustrate you, agitate you, or cause you to all-out explode. Their bothersome behaviors might be repeated. Frustration will follow. Repeat frustration leads to agitation. Repeat agitation leads to explosions. This frustration-agitation-explosion process contributes to the deterioration of your closeness.

Problems in marriage, therefore, need progress and improvement. There is a tool to elicit changes from your spouse without making matters worse as you discuss them. The tool is a script for a Request for Change or Information. This tool simplifies communication so you can get on with the business of enjoying each other and your 7-8-9 relationship. As you follow the script, it will significantly help your spouse with the change process. Because 7-8-9 couples follow rules and use tools, they spend very little time on their problems and most of their time enjoying one another. 0-5s spend much of their time haggling over troubles and dealing with the resulting drama and little time on being buddies.

Often, people will come to therapy and ask me to read a ridiculous amount of text, email, or Facebook "discussions" (fights) they are having with their significant other. They believe I need to see all the details and the "he said"/"she said" arguments in order to get the whole picture. I know they are frustrated, mad, and hurt. The reality is that the reason they are going on and on is because both of them are self-focused.

They are flailing around in their communication, hoping to get some outcome, and frankly, they don't even know what outcome they want. Never, and I mean never, attempt to communicate about important issues via text, email, or social media. Talk on the phone or in person. Use the formats I will show you. Keep things simple, crisp, and clean—not complex, confusing, and messy.

It's important to know that for the most part, people are motivated to change for three reasons.

1. They have the information they need, and they decide to make a change. "Hey, the speed limit is 70. I think I'll start going 70."
2. They change because of love. "I love my children. I need to clean up my life."
3. They change because of pain. "The last time I jumped off the roof with an umbrella, I fractured my ankle. It really hurt. I think I'll put my umbrella away and climb down."

We've all been motivated to change for all three reasons. Each person tends to have a dominant change motivator. What motivates you the most to change? How about your spouse? What motivates him or her to change? When you recognize your spouse's primary change motivator, it will help you understand their inner workings and why they resist certain changes you ask of them.

7-8-9 couples use the Request for Change or Information tool by using information and love as their motivation. 7-8-9s are respectful and kind when they use this script. 0-5 couples often resort to causing their spouse pain to elicit change. For example, they are critical or contemptuous in an attempt to force their spouse to improve. If that doesn't work, they instigate the silent treatment and cause their spouse pain by denying connection and closeness with them. Deterioration is the outcome.

There are five steps to request a change or to ask for information from your spouse. This script, when followed with exactness, bears excellent fruit.

1. Invite your spouse to talk, and preview the subject. "If you have a minute, I'd like to talk to you about _____" (name the subject). Be gentle, specific, and inviting. Never say, "If you have a minute, I'd like to talk to you about something." Defenses go up if an unknown is about to happen. Wait for your spouse to respond that it's a good time to talk.

2. Rate the subject matter on a scale of 1-10 of importance to you. "On a scale of 1-10 of importance to me, it's a 7." Scale the issue honestly in comparison to other issues.

3. Request a change. "Will you help me more with household chores? I'm really exhausted and need some additional help."

Do not give examples or additional reasons why you are asking unless your spouse asks for them. You do not need to "lawyer" why you need the change. These additions just make your communication complex, confusing, and messy. 7-8-9s keep their communication simple, crisp, and clean. Let the request speak for itself. You don't need to prove it is important.

Or, if you are requesting information instead of a change, ask for the information. "Will you help me understand why you are so upset these days? Will you teach me what I can do to help your numbers go up with me?"

4. Listen to your spouse's response. Use cooperative language. Your spouse may say, "I will work on helping more with chores around the house, but maybe we can talk about what tasks would help the most?" In your discussion, use the words "let's," "us," "together," or "we." Sometimes only your spouse needs to change, but often both of you need to work together to get the best outcome. Do not become resolution focused. Keep closeness focused. Work toward a sliver of change to have progress and betterment.

5. Exit successfully. You might say something like, "Thank you for all you do. I know you work hard, and I appreciate your support. You're the best." Remember, the goal is always to end every conversation closer than when you started the conversation. For more difficult issues, it is appropriate to invite your spouse to talk about it again sometime in the future. "Can we talk about this another time?"

Let me remind you of the new culture shift in your marriage. 7-8-9s use the Request for Change or Information tool to eliminate drama from problematic issues. They follow this script. They want their conversation to be delicious, not contentious. They follow the rules and handle issues at frustration level, not agitation or explosion level. They decide beforehand how they will say things. They edit what they say. They slow down. They start their conversations gently. They make requests for change off hot. They don't link issues together. They stay with the subject at hand. They keep the discussion short, between two and five minutes. They are not resolution focused; they are closeness focused. They work toward being closer at the end of the discussion than when they started the discussion. They are self-disciplined. They protect the conversation from themselves and their own misbehavior. They allow restarts if they begin to error. They avoid the war/quit cycle. They manage deterioration with the words they speak. As they maintain closeness throughout their discussion, they trust that the issue at hand will dissolve itself as they protect their 7-8-9 relationship. When they commit to a change, they enthusiastically and quickly make the change they committed to. The issue eventually dissolves, and their closeness improves. Trust increases.

Here's the simple script of a Request for Change or Information.

1) Invite your spouse to talk about a specific subject.
2) Using a 1-10 scale, rate the subject's importance to you.
3) Request the change or the information.
4) Listen to your spouse's response. Use cooperative language. Clarify your meaning lovingly and respectfully.
5) Exit successfully. Compliment and reassure each other of your commitment to a 7-8-9 level of closeness.

One couple I worked with found their courage, and for the first time tried a Request for Change using the script outlined above. After they completed the exercise, the wife, looking a little surprised, turned to me and asked, "Just like that?" She was surprised at the ease of the communication. Before, these talks would almost always end up in a miserable mess. Her husband would go outside all day and poke around. She would do tasks inside to take her mind off the problems. They would try not to cross each other's path. They felt marital depression. After using this script, they learned that communication doesn't need to be a confrontation. "Just like that" can become a powerful moment that results in closeness and progress.

However, if the communication rules we've discussed up to this point are not followed during a Request for Change or Information, you will more than likely fail in that episode. If you do, it's not the end of your life. Try again, and be more disciplined in controlling yourself. Protect the relationship from yourself.

As a therapist, it's magical to watch this script in action. It's even more satisfying to watch it turn into a new pattern of communication for couples. I frequently hear, "Why have we made this so difficult when it is so simple?"

I also hear, "Wow, that was easy!"

One of the more interesting and humorous things I see with couples is their amazement with these discussions, which in the past may have lasted for hours and resulted in a terrible outcome. They remark, "That only took a couple of minutes!"

"Yep," I say, "What are you going to do with the rest of your day? Maybe enjoy each other?"

Chapter 20

Tool #2
Cleanups

"Each person holds so much power within themselves that needs to be let out. Sometimes they just need a little nudge, a little direction, a little support, a little coaching and the greatest things can happen."

– Pete Carroll

I n therapy, I have witnessed that the greatest underlying barrier to marital closeness is a wounded heart that was never fully healed. It is critical to make things right when you have done something to hurt your spouse. Although it would be really cool, this isn't something you can outsource. "Hey Jeff, I'll pay you $50 to apologize to my wife for me. You will? Awesome! I'll give you another $20 if you get it done before the game tonight!"

I spend a lot of time helping couples clean up messes that occurred in the beginning of the marriage or during courtship. Those errors caused bad feelings for years or even decades. I can sometimes see it in their eyes when this has happened. There's a feeling in the room when something is amiss. When I get this sense, I might ask, "Is there something in your marriage that you are having a hard time getting over?" That makes their spouse hold their breath and sphincter tighten. (I know this because they told me later.) A better way would be for you to ask your spouse, "Have I thoroughly cleaned up wrongs that I have done to you?" "Do you harbor resentment or have bad feelings toward me for anything in our past?" These questions require a courageous risk.

I once met with a wife who was very sad because she was not receiving affection from her husband. I asked her if she would ask her husband if there was anything she had done that was keeping him from showing her affection. Shocked, she looked at me and asked, "Are you crazy? That would make things ten times worse!" But after she learned the Cleanup tool, which we'll discuss more in-depth in a moment, she found her courage and asked her husband. It turns out he was withholding because of some things she had done. She did some Cleanups. She returned and surprised me by saying, "I'm so sorry I called you crazy. We had a great talk. Our numbers went way up!" Cleaning up your errors is critical if you want a 7-8-9 marriage. Specific, thorough Cleanups are the way to get the job done.

A quick apology for a heart-wounding error is called a partial Cleanup. It's not complete because there's still a mess left when you are finished. A partial Cleanup would be similar to a heart surgeon who replaces only one valve when two or three others also need to be replaced. "Let's close her up. I'm too scared to do the rest because something bad may happen." A thorough Cleanup requires vulnerability, courage, and a couple more steps.

In many cases, a quick apology is acceptable. "Oops, I forgot to turn off the lights. Sorry about that." There isn't much heart wounding involved in that error. But if an error happens and your spouse was wounded, a quick apology won't do.

"Oops, I forgot you don't like me calling your family leeches and bloodsuckers. Sorry about that. What should we have for lunch?" These are Cleanup efforts you might expect from your goofy friend, but they're not okay coming from your spouse. In this case, a more thorough Cleanup is in order.

A specific Cleanup has an exact script to follow to ensure it's thorough. I encourage you to literally have this script in front of you when you do a Cleanup so you can keep your thoughts straight and have a successful exit. Here it is.

1. Preview. Invite your spouse to talk. "If you have a couple minutes, I'd like to clean up something with you." (Trust me, they will be all ears.)

2. "I recognize I made an error when I _____."
   Don't go too long. Explain your error simply and sincerely.

3. A. Say, "I am sorry," or,
       "I apologize for saying or doing _____."

    B. Claim your baggage.
       "I am responsible for _____."
       (Name the action or words you are claiming ownership of.)

    C. State your plan to change.
       "In the future, I will _____."
       (Name the change specifically.)

4. The receiver of the Cleanup must be open to the Cleanup. If your spouse has just apologized to you, don't say something like, "Whatever," or "I've heard that before!" That's being closed to the Cleanup. Simply absorb it and let it marinate. Forgiveness comes over time and sometimes with layers of Cleanups. Receiving a Cleanup doesn't mean it's done.

Wounds take time and effort to heal. You can also briefly confirm that what your spouse has done did have an impact on you. This isn't where you rub their nose in it to cause them pain. The pain of realizing how their action has affected you and the marriage is sufficient pain.

5. Exit the conversation successfully. What does this mean? Always work to be closer at the end of the conversation than when you started the conversation. "Thank you. I appreciate you seeing your error and apologizing as well as making the necessary changes." "Thank you for receiving my Cleanup. I'll do my best to be better. You're the best."

Here are some additional tips and encouragement about Cleanups.

• Separate your errors like you do your luggage at an airport. Do you claim other people's baggage? Man, I hope not. Claim your own errors and be responsible for them. Let your spouse claim theirs. I would be willing to bet an extra bag of airline peanuts that if you claim your errors more regularly, your spouse will begin to copy your efforts. "You mean if I start cleaning up my mistakes, my spouse will start cleaning up theirs?" Roger that.

• Don't try to clean up all your errors at once. "Sorry for all the bad things I've done our whole relationship. I hope you can forgive me someday." That's not going to fly. If you have done this, you may want to reconsider asking your spouse the questions listed at the beginning of the chapter to see if you have errors that may still need some cleaning up.

• Clean up your errors soon after they happen. If you can't humble yourself right away, then clean up your errors before the next meal. Don't ruin a meal by sitting through it with errors on your mind. Lastly, if those two seem impossible, or if you are letting stubbornness and pride get in the way, find your humility and clean up your error before the end of the day. This is a must for a 7-8-9 marriage. Healthy, happy marriages follow these three timelines (immediately, before a meal, at the end of the day).

- When you finish a Cleanup, don't loop back in and start groveling about how bad you feel or discuss it all over again in that moment. Let it sit and begin to heal. Repeating something does not make it more powerful. It's the sincerity and execution of the plan for change that makes it powerful. Your spouse can recover. They want a better relationship.

- Cleanups should last only about 2-5 minutes. Remember that rule? Always follow the rules when talking.

- I encourage you to promise each other that you'll be open to receiving your spouse's Cleanups. Neither of you will want to do Cleanups if you are afraid they won't be respectfully received.

Don't be the person who hides from the responsibility of cleaning up wounds. Don't rationalize them away or hope they evaporate over time. You must clean up your messes whether they were intentional or accidental. You also need to clean up errors even if you didn't think they were errors. If something you did or said wounded your spouse and you can see it, or if they nudge you and let you know something was hurtful, clean it up. Don't get argumentative or defensive and deny there was a wound. Just seek to understand how it hurt them and go through the script. Your spouse is more than likely going to give you the same respect and grace in the future when they make an error.

I've noticed that some couples keep track of Cleanups. After I taught one couple about Cleanups, the wife said to her husband, "You owe me seven Cleanups for every one Cleanup I do." She had been counting. She probably monitors who picks up what bag at the airport baggage claim as it goes round and round. Do not do this. Just clean up your own errors and claim your own baggage.

Lastly, there is something I call Cleanup preparation. This is used when you are not sure if you've done something to hurt your spouse, or when you sense that you and your spouse don't feel as close. If you are feeling this, you can say something like this:

> "I sense you are kind of distant from me; is that right?"
> "I'm not feeling like we are very close. What's up?"
> "You kind of seem far away. Can we talk a bit?"
> "I don't know if I've done something, but are you
> upset with me?"

In asking these questions, you may find that the problem wasn't caused by you. Whew! If it was you, then you can assess whether you need to do a specific Cleanup or whether your spouse just needs a listening ear.

7-8-9s don't run from the opportunity to help their spouse and marriage. Dive straight in and take a courageous risk. (Use the force, Luke!) It is almost always a bit awkward, scary, and intimidating. Don't cower to these feelings, unless, of course, you want a 0-5 relationship.

Chapter 21

Tool #3
Refuels

*"People need loving the most
when they deserve it the least."*
– John Harrigan

To refuel is, by definition, to supply again with fuel, or, even better, to take on a fresh supply of fuel. Refuels, the most important tool for a 7-8-9 couple, are how 7-8-9s spend most of the time and energy in their relationship. Refuels are the way a couple maintains a 7-8-9 level of closeness. When couples learn that they can manage and control their closeness, rather than just hope it will happen, they become excited about their marriage again. They realize they are not helpless bystanders, doomed to watch their marriage fail. They become the instigator of the kind of marriage they desire. They become hopeful by taking action. By supplying their spouse with Refuels and taking on a fresh supply of Refuels themselves, both are happier.

To "supply again with fuel" is a good way of recognizing that deterioration has taken the fuel that was once there. Maybe I did something wrong by mistake. Maybe it was intentional. Maybe I haven't cleaned up something. Maybe I just haven't done many Refuels or have become lazy in the changes I said I would make. Maybe my spouse just feels distant because we haven't had enough Refuels. Whatever the situation, closeness efforts need to be replenished by you toward your spouse.

Here's a way to find out where your spouse is with you on the closeness scale. I can ask, "What are your numbers these days?" and my spouse may answer, "About a 5." I can simply ask, "What can I do to help you be a 6 or 7 with me?" We don't need to be nuts about moving our closeness level up fast; for example, "What can I do to make it so we are a 10?" We just need to increase by 1 or 2 numbers. Refuels change the direction from a downward trend or stagnation to one of upward movement.

As a marriage therapist, I've learned that most of therapy involves helping couples remember things they used to do but have just forgotten. Yes, I can give new insights from an objective point of view, but what couples need most is a gentle reminder to do the things they used to do that worked. Most couples have sort of turned into Peter Pan and have forgotten how to fly. I guess I'm Tinker Bell (of the masculine type, of course), and with my dry erase wand, I just show them the steps. When they remember, I watch them wake up right in front of me.

I can almost guarantee that when a couple comes in to their first session, they have abandoned one very special action that got them interested in each other in the first place. They have quit greeting each other.

Greetings have three components:

1. Eye contact
2. Smile
3. Physical touch (no groping, fellas)

One easy assignment, then, is to start greeting each other again. When you come home, or when you cross paths in the house, you can greet your spouse with these three quick Refuels. It takes only seconds.

If I'm at a 0-5 level of closeness with my spouse, I'm probably beginning to be "allergic" to them. I will decrease or stop eye contact, or I will stop smiling at them, and I will probably avoid touching them. Other types of Refuels may also decrease. If I quit doing Refuels long enough, it could mean an end of the relationship. Reversing this behavior, and making an effort to make eye contact with, smile at, and touch my spouse tells my spouse that I like and want them and desire to be close to them. It's a great start. When I change the pattern from Refuel neglect to Refuel abundance, I change the whole experience I have with my spouse. I am now able to determine and control what kind of relationship I want every day. Pride and stubbornness are my only barriers.

"To take on a fresh supply of fuel" means to receive Refuels and not reject them because of pride or stubbornness. 7-8-9 couples always welcome the positive efforts of their spouse. 0-5 couples resist Refuels or make it difficult for their spouse to Refuel them. They have become comfortable in being complacent.

Sometimes a Refuel involves using the Cleanup tool or taking positive action steps using the Request for Change tool. Most of the time, however, Refuels involve acts of service, kind and loving gestures, gift giving, positive communication, dating experiences or outings, affection, sex, and a host of other things learned by teaching and training each other.

Simply put, Refuels can be shown by changing negative behavior into positive behavior. Some things you do may give your spouse the impression you don't care about them as much as you actually do. One wife said to her husband, "Hey, maybe you could quit eating on the couch while you watch football and instead come and eat with me in the dining room sometimes. That would make a difference in how much I think you like me."

In grade school, I got one of the coolest Refuels. A super cute girl I had a serious crush on occupied all my thinking. I couldn't keep my eyes off her. She noticed my interest and reciprocated just a little. One day, she passed a paper to her friend, who then passed it on to me. The note simply said, "Do you like me? Yes [ ] or No [ ]". I checked the appropriate box and passed the note back and watched for her reaction. She looked at me and smiled. Now *that* was a Refuel I've remembered forever. I did nothing with this information due to sheer terror, but nonetheless, it was an awesome 10 Refuel. I guess I can happily say I had one brief relationship that was always a 10.

All Refuels are good, but some Refuels are especially delicious. You get to decide how many and to what intensity you have Refuels in your marriage. You may be thinking, "Not my wife or husband — I've tried everything!" I can assure you that everyone wants Refuels and wants to be wanted. You just don't fully know what your spouse's Refuels are yet. The key is to let them teach and train you with exactness. The following exercise will help you learn what a "10" Refuel is to your spouse. If you are courageous enough to complete this exercise, you and your spouse will both benefit.

Make a bullseye. Put the number 10 in the center and the number 1 as the outside ring. A 1 represents a minor Refuel to gain closeness, and a 10 is as close as you can feel to your spouse in the moment. See if you can guess three 10s of your spouse. Let them rate the Refuel between 1 and 10 after you guess each one.

For example, I may guess, "I take you to dinner and a movie and have dessert afterwards with no kids."

My spouse would then tell me what number that would be for her. "That would be a 9," she may say.

Then, I guess two more Refuels, attempting to hit a 10. After each guess, my wife would rate what the actual value of the Refuel would be for her. Following these three guesses, she teaches me three more 10s for her. Then we switch, and my spouse guesses as I rate them, and then I teach her three more Refuels that would represent 10s for me. Remember, any number on the Refuel scale is a Refuel. They just vary in importance. It is amazing to find that most couples struggle to know what their spouse's 10s are, yet they expect that their spouse should know what would constitute a 10 for them. After you have each taken a turn, ask each other two questions:

• What did you learn about me from this?
• What did you learn about yourself from this?

Exploration brings eroticism to the marriage. Eroticism is an essential component to a 7-8-9 relationship.

Why is it so important to learn your spouse's Refuel importance? Because you want to fulfill their needs to be desired and taken care of. Let them teach you how to accomplish this. This is as close to their operation manual as you can get. Your spouse is going to make it easy work for you.

When your spouse is feeling like a 7-8-9, they will be looking to help you be a 7-8-9 with them. When you reciprocate this action, you cross-pollinate each other. Don't make your Refuels too far apart. Refuels should be done daily. By the way, I encourage all my couples to date weekly. 7-8-9s consistently work on Refuels. Unhealthy couples think resolving their differences is the way to be close. In the process, they cross-contaminate each other with the war/quit cycle.

7-8-9 couples love to put their time and energy into Refuels. They are in perpetual motion, working to go toward their spouse. They are highly aware of their spouse's needs and actively pursue closeness with them through action. They are not apathetic in their relationship. They are thriving and feeling wonderful in their heads, hearts, and stomachs. They are doing the easy work of a 7-8-9 relationship.

      TOOL 1. REQUEST FOR CHANGE OR INFORMATION
      TOOL 2. CLEANUPS
      TOOL 3. REFUELS

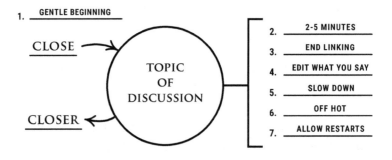

Chapter 22

7-8-9 Sexual Intimacy

"The functional benefits of couple sexuality are to create shared pleasure, reinforce and deepen intimacy, and serve as a tension reducer to deal with the stresses of life and marriage."

– Barry and Emily McCarthy

I would like to tell you that having a close, 7-8-9 relationship will make awesome sex happen, but it won't. Of course, love and closeness are important ingredients of great sex, but just as love is not sufficient to make closeness consistent, closeness is not sufficient to ensure a great sex life.

There is something you can always count on, however, when trying to figure out your spouse and sex, and that is this: everyone wants to be wanted and desired. Going with that assumption, you will need your spouse to tell you what being wanted and desired means to them, both in and out of the bedroom.

A great way to start a discussion about sex is to do this simple Q and A exercise with each other. Using an A, B, C, D, F grading system, take turns interviewing (not interrogating!) each other, using the following questions. Each section of the discussion should last no more than two to five minutes. Be a good listener, not an arguer. There is no need to resolve your sexual issues as you talk. Instead, seek to understand, explore, and be curious.

Use humor, but be productive. Allow vulnerability by taking a courageous risk. Don't be easily offended. The purpose of this exercise is to get to know your spouse with the hope of progress and betterment, not perfection.

Section 1. Ask your spouse the following:

- How would you grade the quality of our sex?
- How would you grade the quantity of our sex?
- How would you grade the duration of our sex?

Then ask:

- What would a better quality be like for you?
- What is a desirable quantity?
- What would you like to see differently pertaining to duration?

Section 2. Assess what percentage of time you spend in each of these areas as a couple.

- What percentage of our sex is quickie sex?
- What percentage of our sex is moderate sex?
- What percentage of our sex is deep, intimate sex?

Briefly discuss what each area means to you and how it could be better.

After each of you has taken a turn discussing these topics, talk about one or two things you are personally willing to change to help make sexuality a little better for your spouse. Actively follow through with what you say you are going to do. At the end of the discussion, each spouse should give the other two compliments on what they do well sexually.

Years ago, I received some great counsel from a therapist about how much sex a couple should have. He said, "A little less than one of you thinks and a little more than one of you thinks." Work toward better sexual compatibility, not just fulfillment of your own fantasies.

Making your needs and wants known about sexuality through teaching and training each other will positively influence 7-8-9 sexuality. You gotta wanna have a great intimate relationship; it's not going to happen automatically.

Research has shown that sexuality comprises only about 10-15% of a marriage relationship. However, if the 10-15% isn't going well, it affects the other 85-90% of the relationship negatively. Don't be that couple.

I have listened countless times to what happens when a man or woman is rejected sexually by their spouse. They have two general responses.

1. They withdraw.
2. They get irritable and do very little of what their
   spouse wants them to do.

Resentment builds. Deterioration increases. If you don't like these outcomes, have brief but frequent, gentle, and kind talks about sex and how each of you can improve what you are doing. Hint: If these discussions involve blaming each other, nothing will change.

Poor communication about sex disables a marital relationship. Without discussion and action, couples remain unfulfilled and resentful. It may feel like driving around with your parking brake on or dragging an anchor behind a boat. It will slow your ability to move forward as a 7-8-9 couple. It more than likely will keep you in the 4-5-6 range at best.

When a couple comes in to therapy and they are in the 1-6 range, I can almost always assume that sex is not where it needs to be for either person. Communication between them about the topic is usually at a very novice level. I have talked to many couples who have been married over 30 years who have never had a significant discussion about their sexual lives together. Instead of having an ongoing discussion, they have fallen into the war/quit cycle.

It is not an option to have a limited sex or sexless marriage, unless both of you want it that way. Those couples might exist, but I have personally never talked to one. In all other cases, if you are the person in the relationship who has justified, rationalized, controlled, limited, manipulated, or avoided working on or improving the sexual relationship, you must end this negative thinking and associated behaviors and find a way to progress. It's your responsibility to initiate and encourage the change. I'm not suggesting that your spouse wasn't part of this problem. Both of you probably contributed. All I can tell you is this: one of you is feeling neglected and deprived, and one of you wants to be left alone. Does this sound like a 7-8-9 marriage, or something else?

There are endless articles, videos, blogs, and books to help couples find greater sexual fulfillment. Saying "I don't care" or "I don't know what to do anymore" are not justifiable answers to the problem. Giving up or just surviving is not fair to you, your spouse, or your marriage. Begin to communicate using the suggestions in this chapter. Follow the rules and tools as you talk. Go toward your spouse and do a cleanup if you need to. Ask to work with your spouse to improve your sexual closeness with the goal that both of you can find fulfillment. If you need to talk with a professional to work through things that cause you to have a negative attitude about sexuality, do it. You will find that the results will be beneficial to all aspects of your relationship.

The purpose of this book is to help couples sustain a 7-8-9 relationship, mostly through communicative practices and techniques. As you seek a 7-8-9 relationship, it is critical to keep learning about your own and your spouse's sexuality, because it evolves through the years.

An excellent resource that I recommend you read together is Barry and Emily McCarthy's *Rekindling Desire* (2nd edition, 2014). As experts in the field, the McCarthys do a wonderful job of presenting all the information you will need to build an intimate sexual team. Their focus on desire, pleasure, eroticism, satisfaction, and everything in between makes for an informative read that will help your intimate progress.

7-8-9 couples work toward a close sexual connection. They are seeking to thrive in all they do individually and as a couple. 0-3s have all but given up on intimacy. 4-5-6s have become apathetic about it. 7-8-9s are always seeking the "10" moments. You are 7-8-9 capable.

Chapter 23

The Simple Secret of Happy Veteran Marriages

Wizard of Oz: As for you,
my galvanized friend, you want a heart.
You don't know how lucky you are not to have one.
Hearts will never be practical until
they can be made unbreakable.
Tin Man: But I still want one.

When problems arise in a relationship and a couple starts to focus on resolving those problems instead of focusing on closeness, their communication becomes dysfunctional. Typically, there is one individual in the relationship who is more likely to push for resolution. It isn't gender specific; rather, it is driven by the person who has the stronger philosophy that the solution to marital distance is to resolve problems. This resolution focus might work if both people are on board and never act out, and if neither person displays resistance to the needs and wants of their spouse. Maybe it would work in Utopia, but most couples don't live by Utopian standards.

Many years ago, I worked with a veteran couple – a couple with over 20 years of marriage under their belt. This husband and wife had been married for 42 years. The husband had worked for NASA, and he and his wife had raised five children to adulthood.

They felt very good about all they had done and were enjoying their retirement. They had never been in marriage therapy before coming to see me, and I worked with them for just one session. Working with this couple was a highlight in my career; they taught me more in one session than I could have taught them in 20 sessions.

The husband had made the appointment. His chief complaint, and the reason for coming to see a professional, was his wife's attitude. He had been retired for 20 years and was one of many engineers who had contributed to the moon landing. He had loved his career choice and his employer. He told me that NASA eventually planned to have a base on the moon and establish a colony of professionals there for research purposes. Ideally, their spouses would be with them in this colony.

One day this man was talking with his wife about his old job and how he missed it. A discussion came up about the moon colony. He told his wife how disappointed he was that he wasn't younger, because if he were, he could have gone to the moon with her to be part of the future colony. He even told her that if they colonized the moon now, he would go, and he wanted her to go with him. Her response rattled him to the core. He was stunned and upset when his wife told him, "I wouldn't have gone with you to the moon even if we could have gone years ago, and I wouldn't go now."

He could not believe what he had heard. He was shocked to learn that his wife wouldn't have supported him in his career dreams, of which he had been so proud. He took her answer extremely hard. It felt marriage threatening and caused him to question the trust he had in her and her support all these years. He said to me, "I thought I knew her all these years, but I guess I didn't." He then said, "I don't know if I would have married her if I knew that in the end she wouldn't have supported me in that decision." He was deeply hurt by her lack of commitment.

According to them, for the first time in their marriage, they had not been communicating for about two weeks because of this horrible revelation. They had deteriorated to about a 3 level of closeness. They were both miserable and didn't know what to do.

After hearing their story, I asked the old gentleman to step out and let me speak to his wife alone for a few minutes. He did so willingly, and as he left, he said timidly, "I don't know if it's possible, but I hope you can talk some sense into her."

I tried to contain my laughter at the whole scenario. "Be patient with him," I thought to myself, "He is an engineer and has a particular view of life."

When he left the room, I asked this wonderful woman a few questions. "Is it true that you would not have gone to the moon with him?"

She smiled and answered, "Yes."

"Will you explain why you wouldn't?"

Smiling, she said, "I wouldn't want to be away from my family. I wouldn't want to raise children up there. I wouldn't want to be up there for hundreds of reasons. Would you?"

I answered, "Well, no, I wouldn't either." Then I asked, "Do you love your husband?"

She replied with a smile, "Oh, yes. He is my best friend. He has been a wonderful provider and father. I feel terrible that he's upset about this silly topic."

Then I asked, "Why are you coming to see a therapist now, about this particular issue, when you made it through all the decisions and difficulties of raising a family together without the need for professional help?"

She replied, "Because my husband is stuck on this issue."

Without realizing it, she then told me the secrets of veteran couples, and for that matter, the secrets all couples must incorporate into their marriage if the marriage is to be successful. Following the rules and tools we have discussed up to this point is necessary, of course, but in the end, the secrets this woman told me must be applied so that couples can navigate all the remaining issues.

She said, "I've learned to *adjust* to many, many things that won't change. I've learned to *adapt* to situations as they come because they require it. I've learned that a happy and successful marriage requires each spouse to make *accommodations* for the other."

I then asked her, "Do you really think NASA will be colonizing the moon in your lifetime?"

She laughed and said, "Of course not!"

I then asked her, "How can you apply the principles you just explained to me to this current situation so that you and your husband will remain good friends?"

After thinking for a moment, she replied, "I know what to say."

I then invited her husband back into the room, and she scooted close to him and held his hand. She then said, "Oh, Robert [not his real name], I have thought it over, and I have decided that if NASA wants you to help colonize the moon, I will go. I think it isn't likely, but if it does happen, I would want to be with you because you are my best friend. The thought of living on earth without my best friend would be miserable. In fact, it has been miserable for the last two weeks. I don't like how I am feeling, and I don't think you do either. There's no need to fight about this anymore. Let's go eat lunch."

He smiled at her and kissed her, and while looking at me, said, "I don't know what you did, but you did your job well!" They stood up, and as they were walking out, the wife looked back at me and winked, and off they went.

I never saw them again. Many years have gone by, and I believe they have both passed away. I have thought of them periodically over the years, and as of this writing, I am kind of thinking they have visited the moon, where they are holding hands and laughing about their earth life adventures.

What great counsel to every couple who wants a 7-8-9 relationship. If you aren't willing to do the three things this beautiful couple taught me, then you will probably have a 0-5 relationship. Without these mature skills, you might live with resentment, anger, and spite. Don't do that. Be like this wonderful veteran couple and realize that a successful, happy, 7-8-9 marriage requires couples to –

- adjust to things that won't change,
- adapt to situations as they come, and
- accommodate each other.

CPSIA information can be obtained
at www.ICGtesting.com
Printed in the USA
LVHW101415210419
614941LV00011BA/141/P

9 780692 969366